TAKE AND EAT:
LIVING EUCHARISTICALLY

TAKE AND EAT: LIVING EUCHARISTICALLY

Msgr. Joseph DeGrocco

Resurrection Press

An Imprint of
CATHOLIC BOOK PUBLISHING CORP.
Totowa • New Jersey

First published in September 2010 by

    Catholic Book Publishing/Resurrection Press

    77 West End Road

    Totowa, NJ 07512

ISBN 978-1-933066-12-7

Library of Congress Catalog Card Number: 2010928255

Mass texts quoted in this book reflect the most recent translation of the Roman Missal. Although as of this writing the Missal has not yet gone into effect, the new translation of the Eucharistic Prayers has received the *recognitio* from Rome. The texts of the Roman Missal used herein are taken from http://www.usccb.org/romanmissal/

Cover design by Geoffrey Butz

Printed in the United States of America

www.catholicbookpublishing.com

Dedication

To my parents, William S. and Marsille DeGrocco,
who taught me about eucharistic living
with the bread and wine
and the
taking, blessing, breaking, and giving
of our family life.

༼ɔ◞ɔ

Contents

Introduction

I LOVE liturgy! Ever since my early days in seminary formation studying for the priesthood, I have loved the study of the liturgy. I am thrilled and privileged that I had the opportunity to do graduate studies in liturgy, and I love my current priestly assignment as Professor of Liturgy and Director of Liturgical Formation at the Seminary of the Immaculate Conception in Huntington, New York, teaching both seminarians and lay people about liturgy. I want others to love it and understand it too.

This book is intended to help people enter more deeply into the Church's liturgical celebration of the Eucharist. The text has been written as a series of spiritual meditations geared toward the "people in the pew," not only to help them participate more fully in the Mass, but also to gain a deeper appreciation of how eucharistic spirituality can be integrated into everyday life. I am convinced that one of the great challenges—as we continue into the 21st century—is that of helping Catholics to more deeply understand what true participation in the Mass is all about, a participation that is limited not only to the celebration of the ritual but extends into the way we live our Catholic Christian life.

This book, then, is not a treatise about the theological meaning of the parts of the Mass; it will not walk you through the entire Mass, although certain parts of the Mass will be discussed. Instead, through a series of reflections structured around the eucharistic actions of taking, blessing, breaking, and giving, the reader will, it is hoped, be brought to reflect more deeply on themes such as our full participation in the celebration of the Eucharist, the transformation of our life to reflect the life of Jesus more completely, and the connection between what we celebrate at Mass with the everyday journey of our life.

So this book is really about liturgy and life, specifically, about making the spiritual connections between the two. There will be stories to try to exemplify and highlight relevant spiritual themes; some stories will be humorous and some will be serious. Some will be personal, using examples from my own life as a Catholic and as a priest. Many of the stories will use everyday images, sometimes using images or incidents taken from popular culture to highlight a spiritual point. The reflections are taken from real life because our faith should always be about real life, since, ultimately, that is where real eucharistic living occurs.

I have resisted the urge to do a great deal of teaching in these pages. Although structured around the four eucharistic actions of taking, blessing, breaking, and giving, the content is not so much a systematic presentation as much as it is a deepening spiral, with those four actions as reference points. As a deepening spiral, it will keep revisiting certain themes that run throughout these pages: what it means to live eucharistically; how to connect liturgy and everyday life; what it means to offer ourselves to God the Father in union with Jesus at Mass and in everyday life; how to transform our life into a deeper Christian life; how to unite ourselves with Jesus.

It is hoped these reflections will spur further reflections. Perhaps parts of this book can be used to prepare for Mass; perhaps sections can be used as food for thought after Mass. Discussion and faith-sharing groups might find this book useful for their meetings. Reflections are often broken down using subheadings and can be used either as they appear or in no particular sequence. If these reflections assist homilists in preparing their homilies, then that is all to the good as well.

Everyday life is where it all happens, and so that is the focus of these reflections. The subtext of this work is that we want to get our celebration of liturgy right so we can get our celebration of life right, and in order to get liturgy right, we have to be getting Christian life right. After all, *liturgy is life and life is liturgical!*

November 9, 2009
Feast of the Dedication of the
Lateran Basilica in Rome

1

COMING TO THE EUCHARIST

❧

ALLOW me to tell a personal story to get us started.

Anyone who knows me knows that I am, as they say, "heavy into Superman." I love everything about the character and the legend, the fantasy and the heroics. This fascination with Superman is nothing new. Even as a child I would play Superman and dream of being faster than a speeding bullet, more powerful than a locomotive, and able to leap tall buildings in a single bound.

In fact, when I was about age 6 or 7, I thought it would be so great to be Superman that I prayed to God to give me superpowers. It would have been wonderful to be able to do the things Superman could do, and the request was not entirely selfish, since I was more than willing to use my powers to fight for truth, justice, and the American way.

Since I could never be sure exactly when God would answer my request, I had to keep checking. Fortunately, I had the presence of mind not to jump off any rooftops to see if I could fly! Instead, I would sit and stare at the wall to see if I could see through it with my newly-acquired X-ray vision. Or, when no one was looking, I would try to lift the living room couch with one hand to test for super-strength.

Well, needless to say, I never was able to see through the wall or lift the couch. Weeks later, in my disappointment, I confided to my mother this secret request to God. Her response was something which was lost on me at the time, but has nonetheless stayed with me ever since. Her response was, "Joe,

God couldn't possibly grant your request, because if He did, you would no longer be human; you would no longer be YOU."

By now you're probably asking yourself, *What does this story have to do with a book about the spirituality of the Eucharist?*

Celebrating the Eucharist is the most important thing we do as Catholic Christians. It's something that should be at the center of our life and the center of our prayer and spirituality. The riches and blessings we partake of in celebrating the Eucharist are innumerable. We know that we encounter Jesus as He is present to us in the gathered assembly, in the Word, and in His Real Presence in the Sacred Species of His Body and Blood. We know that intimate union with Him is given to us as He feeds us with the gift of His Risen Body and Blood. We know that we find healing, forgiveness, and new life every time we share in the Eucharist.

But Eucharist should do something else for us as well—it should help us to become who we are and who we are meant to be—and it should help us to do that because of what we bring to the Eucharist.

What do we become? The answer to that can be found in the New Testament's first letter of Peter: "You are a chosen race, a royal priesthood, a holy nation, a people set apart. Once you were not a people at all, and now you are the People of God" (2:9-11). That's the truth of who we are—the truth of what makes you, you; me, me; and us, us.

I believe that the action of becoming who we are is central to our participation in the Eucharist. I fear that sometimes we approach the Eucharist too passively, as though the focus for our participating in this great sacrament were merely a matter of "receiving." True, we do "receive" Holy Communion, but not in any passive sense. Our reception of Holy Communion is meant to be a key moment in our ongoing active relationship with the Lord Jesus. That act of receiving Holy Communion has at its heart Jesus Who gives Himself to us completely and Who asks for a giving on our part as well, a commitment to His life and His way, an openness to continually become who and what He has called us to be.

This was a favorite theme of St. Augustine's (AD 354-430). In a famous homily, Augustine preached these words:

> The reason these things, brothers and sisters, are called sacraments is that in them one thing is seen, another is to be understood. What can be seen has a bodily appearance, what is to be understood provides spiritual fruit. So if you want to understand the body of Christ, listen to the apostle telling the faithful, *You, though, are the body of Christ and its members* (1 Cor 12:27). So if it's you that are the body of Christ and its members, it's the mystery meaning you that has been placed on the Lord's table; what you receive is the mystery that means you. It is to what you are that you reply *Amen*, and by so replying you express your assent. What you hear, you see, is *The body of Christ*, and you answer, *Amen*. So be a member of the body of Christ, in order to make that *Amen* true.[1]

What it means to participate in the Eucharist as an action that makes us who we are, and as an action that helps us to live differently, is one of the central themes of this book as we explore a spirituality of the Eucharist.

---

[1] Rotelle, John E. O.S.A., ed. *The Works of St. Augustine: A Translation for the 21st Century*. Translation and notes by Edmund Hill, O.P. (New Rochelle: New City Press, 1993), p. 300.

Who we are called to be

The truth of who we are, who we are called to be, and who we are called to become by doing what we do at the celebration of the Eucharist was brought home to me while I was distributing Holy Communion at Mass during my first year of priesthood. Before me came a little boy, seven, maybe eight years of age. "The Body of Christ," I said to him, holding up a host. Then, with arms outstretched and a grin as wide as his face would hold, he replied, "I am."

Now, my first reaction was, "How cute! He meant to say, 'Amen,' and he got the word wrong." But then I thought about it. What if he didn't get it wrong? What if that little boy knew exactly what he was saying? What a profound understanding of the Eucharist: "The Body of Christ . . . I am/we are!" That's the truth of who you and I are and who we are called to become by doing what we do at Mass; it's the key to recognizing the presence of Jesus Christ—a presence that calls us to enter into a deeper relationship with Him—by bringing the gift of ourselves to Eucharist.

If we are truly going to recognize Him in our celebration of the Eucharist, then we have to ask some very pointed questions about what we do at Eucharist, questions that touch on the very meaning of what it means to participate in the celebration of the Eucharist. These are questions that cut to the heart of the matter, questions like: *What do we do when we celebrate the Eucharist? Is the Eucharist just a thing, an object to be passively received? Or, is it an action, celebrated by a kingdom of priests, celebrating who we are and whose we are, what we bring and what we are called to become?*

Participation at Mass—Internal and External

The Second Vatican Council, in *Sacrosanctum Concilium,* the Constitution on the Sacred Liturgy, gave us this vision for the

Church's celebration of liturgy, a vision that especially applies to the celebration of the Eucharist as described in paragraph 14:

> Mother Church earnestly desires that all the faithful should be led to that full, conscious and active participation in liturgical celebrations which is demanded by the very nature of the liturgy, and to which the Christian people, "a chosen race, a royal priesthood, a holy nation, a redeemed people" (1 Pet 2:9, 4-5) have a right and obligation by reason of their baptism. In the restoration and promotion of the sacred liturgy the full and active participation by all the people is the aim to be considered before all else, for it is the primary and indispensable source from which the faithful are to derive the true Christian spirit.[2]

If we are truly going to fully, consciously, and actively participate in the celebration of the Eucharist and allow that sacrament to help us become who God calls us to be, then we must understand the difference between receiving a thing and celebrating an action, and we must have the proper understanding of what that action is and how we actively participate. There are two aspects to that active participation: the action at Mass, and the action outside of Mass.

The Council called us to "full, conscious and active" participation in the action at Mass, but we should not misunderstand the meaning of "active." We might associate "active" simply with external action, and while our participation at Mass certainly involves external actions, that's only part of it; the action of participating at Mass also involves the internal component. In fact, to truly have "full, conscious and active participation," we must be doing both internal and external participation. The

---

[2] Flannery, Austin, ed. *Vatican II: The Conciliar and Post Conciliar Documents* (Northport: Costello Publishing Company, 1975).

two are related and mutually reinforce each other. The full spiritual benefits of participating in Mass are not being realized if we are not participating in both ways, externally and internally.

External participation is easy to describe. By external participation we mean all of the outward things we do at Mass: the verbal responses—both spoken and sung—the standing, sitting, kneeling, joining in processions. All the things we do with our bodies are part of the external participation, and if we are not doing them then we are not participating as fully as we should. You may think you are participating because you are attentive to what's going on, or you may have a holy feeling (a sense of God's presence), but full participation can only be achieved through the mutual interaction between our interior self and our exterior self. Participation in the communal action that is the Eucharist is never just a matter of what an individual is feeling on the inside.

Neither is someone fully participating who joins in the spoken responses but not in the singing. Sometimes we'll use the excuse, "I can't sing," or "I don't like to sing." The fact is, though, that it's not about any one of us and what we like or don't like to do. When we are at Mass we all have the responsibility to participate fully, so whether or not we like to sing is irrelevant; it's part of the definition of what we are supposed to do just by virtue of being there. Besides, as I always say, if God gave you a lousy singing voice, then He deserves to hear it directed back at Him loudly and proudly!

At the same time, we must also understand that our exterior actions do not complete our participation; there also has to be an interior component. The person who participates completely and enthusiastically in all the spoken and sung responses and in all the bodily movements and gestures still may not be participating fully if that person is not spiritually attentive and internally focused on what is going on. The external is important because it stimulates and nourishes the internal; the outer must make its way inward. This interior component of liturgical participation, in fact, reminds us that true participation is not a matter of "how much" one does at Mass, but rather how well one does all of what one is supposed to do and how attentive one is to doing it.

This is where I fear that sometimes we have a mistaken notion of participation being related solely to the external—the more one can "get up and do" at Mass the more one is participating. For example, when liturgical ministers such as lectors, extraordinary ministers of Holy Communion, or cantors are asked what they like about being a minister, often they answer, "I like it because I feel like I am participating more." This is actually a mistaken notion, however. Full participation is not dependent on how much we "get up and do." The "person in the pew" who does nothing more than participate in all the responses, spoken and sung, and all the gestures and postures proper to the members of the assembly, can be participating just as much as the priest, as long as that person is doing them with full engagement and attentiveness. "Full, conscious and active participation" means doing all the ritual actions one is supposed to do and, in doing them, thus encountering the mystery that is being made present through that ritual enactment. In fact, if the priest is distracted during Mass, not giving himself over totally to the sacred actions he is enacting, the "person in the pew" might be participating more than the priest in the true meaning of what liturgical participation is all about!

Everyone participates equally in the sacred action according to their role. The liturgical assembly, the body of Christ, is a structured organism made up of a diversity of roles and gifts, all united in Christ and in their common action but all sharing in it in different ways. The differences do not mean that any one role is "higher" or better or more intrinsically holy; no one role is closer to Christ. Together, the liturgical assembly, i.e., priest and people, are the body of Christ. The priest has the unique and irreplaceable role as presider of imaging and being the icon of Christ, the Head of the Body, and together with the assembly, images the Body of Christ. Jesus Christ is present in various ways throughout the liturgy, one and the same presence experienced in different modes at different times. Again we can look to *Sacrosanctum Concilium*, the Liturgy Constitution of Vatican II, this time to paragraph 7:

> To accomplish so great a work Christ is always present in his Church, especially in her liturgical celebrations. He is present in the Sacrifice of the Mass not only in the person of his minister, "the same now offering, through the ministry of priests, who formerly offered himself on the cross," but especially in the Eucharistic species. By his power he is present in the sacraments so that when anybody baptizes it is really Christ himself who baptizes. He is present in his word since it is he himself who speaks when the holy scriptures are read in the Church. Lastly, he is present when the Church prays and sings, for he has promised "where two or three are gathered together in my name there am I in the midst of them" (Mt 18:20).
>
> Christ, indeed, always associates the Church with himself in this great work in which God is perfectly glorified and men are sanctified. The Church is his beloved Bride who calls to her Lord, and through him offers worship to the eternal Father.

The liturgy, then, is rightly seen as an exercise of the priestly office of Jesus Christ. It involves the presentation of man's sanctification under the guise of signs perceptible by the senses and its accomplishment in ways appropriate to each of these signs. In it full public worship is performed by the Mystical Body of Jesus Christ, that is, by the Head and his members.[3]

Clearly, then, every liturgical action is an action of the body, the entire assembly. First and foremost, of course, it is an action of Christ, but it is Christ as He is present in His body, the Church. Liturgical celebrations are not actions of the priest that the people follow; they are actions of the body in which all act according to their role. In the case of the celebration of the Eucharist, everyone enters into the action of offering the sacrifice. Paragraph 48 of the Constitution on the Sacred Liturgy explains it this way:

The Church, therefore, earnestly desires that Christ's faithful, when present at this mystery of faith, should not be there as strangers or silent spectators. On the contrary, through a good understanding of the rites and prayers they should take part in the sacred action, conscious of what they are doing, with devotion and full collaboration. They should be instructed by God's word, and be nourished at the table of the Lord's Body. They should give thanks to God. **Offering the Immaculate Victim, not only through the hands of the priest but also together with him, they should learn to offer themselves. Through Christ the mediator, they should be drawn day by day into ever more perfect union with God and each other, so that finally God may be all in all.**[4] (emphasis added)

---

[3] Ibid.
[4] Ibid.

There it is: there is the central action that we all participate in equally, that of offering. Offering is connected to remembering, which we all do. The *General Instruction of the Roman Missal*, in paragraph 79, makes explicit the connection between remembering and offering (actually quoting the Liturgy Constitution) when it describes the part of the Eucharistic Prayer called the *anamnesis*, a part of the prayer that is easily identifiable by its explicitation of the action "we remember, therefore we offer":

> . . . the Church, fulfilling the command that she received from Christ the Lord through the Apostles, keeps the memorial of Christ, recalling especially his blessed Passion, glorious Resurrection, and Ascension into heaven…[I]n this very memorial, the Church—and in particular the Church here and now gathered—offers in the Holy Spirit the spotless Victim to the Father. The Church's intention, however, is that the faithful not only offer this spotless Victim but **also learn to offer themselves, and so day by day to be consummated, through Christ the mediator, into unity with God and with each other, so that at last God may be all in all.**[5] (emphasis added)

It is in the Eucharistic Prayer that the Church remembers and makes present Christ's sacrifice. Everyone gathered at the Eucharist joins in praying the Eucharistic Prayer: the priest prays the prayer in the name of (but not in place of) the people, articulating his parts out loud; the people join in the prayer through their internal participation of offering themselves and uniting to Christ, and through their external participation of articulating their parts, namely, the responses, the Holy, Holy

---

[5] Liturgy Documentary Series 2, United States Conference of Catholic Bishops (Washington D.C., 2003).

(the *Sanctus*), the Memorial Acclamation, and, most importantly, the Great Amen. The connection between the Eucharistic
Prayer and the eucharistic life revolves around what the
General Instruction tells us in the quotation cited above: the
faithful should not only offer the spotless victim at Mass, but,
in so doing, should learn to offer themselves in union with
Christ, so that, in a life of offering lived in union with Christ
and with each other, every member of the body of Christ gives
witness to God's presence everywhere.

This eucharistic reality of offering ourselves day by day
through Christ, with Him and in Him, so that we may be united more deeply with Him, and offering ourselves to Him by
offering ourselves in self-giving love to our brothers and sisters, thus being more deeply united with them, is the heart of a
eucharistic spirituality; this is the place where internal and
external participation meet; this is the place where what we do
at Mass connects with the way we conduct our life outside of
Mass; this is what it means to live eucharistically. This is where
we are challenged to allow the celebration of the Eucharist to
connect to our everyday life, as we more and more become
who we are and who we are called to be.

Participation outside Mass

To really live eucharistically, we must see the connection
between our celebration of the Eucharist and the Christian life we
live every day; we must recognize His presence at Mass because
we also recognize Him present to us outside of Mass. We can recognize Him at Mass if we are doing the action that we do together at Mass through Him, with Him, and in Him as an action connected to becoming who we are called to be in everyday life. It all
gets back to that sense of connectedness. Connected to what? To
the body! *The Body of Christ . . . I am/we are!*

It is this action of living eucharistically that is at the heart of what we celebrate every time we celebrate the Eucharist. Therefore, the Body and Blood of Christ should not just be something we receive, but rather it should be an action that causes us to become what we share. It should be an action of being transformed into that reality. We fully recognize Jesus as He is present at the Eucharist and as He is present to us in our everyday life because we are members of His body.

How can we further explore how the Eucharist molds us and forms us into who we already are as His body? Well, we can start by considering my three favorite movies of all time: the first-place choice should be no surprise as it is *Superman: The Movie* (1978); in second place is *Casablanca* (1942); and in third place *The Wizard of Oz* (1939). Strange as it may sound, it is *The Wizard of Oz* that can help to shed some light on this dynamic connection of being formed and molded into eucharistic living through our celebration of the Eucharist in church.

Recall, if you will, the four main characters in *The Wizard of Oz*: Dorothy, the Scarecrow, the Tin Man, and the Cowardly Lion. They were all on a journey (a pilgrimage, you might say) to find the Wizard because they were all in search of something. Dorothy was looking to go back home to Kansas; the Scarecrow wanted a brain; the Tin Man yearned for a heart; and the Cowardly Lion needed courage.

Here's the catch: When they finally meet up with the Wizard, did they receive what they were looking for? Did the Wizard really give them something they didn't already have? No! He points out that what they were looking for was with them all along; they just didn't know it. Nonetheless, he does give them all something. He gives the Scarecrow a diploma; he gives the Tin Man a testimonial; he gives the Cowardly Lion a medal. In addition, Glinda, the Good Witch, tells Dorothy that the power to go home was always with her in her ruby slippers, but she had to discover it for herself. All she had to do was click her heels together three times and say, "There's no place like home." Each of them had what they needed and wanted all along, but they needed something to act as a trigger so that what they had could become effective and make a difference in their life. In other words, they needed some symbol to help them sacramentalize the reality that was already in their midst.

This is a great reminder to us of the importance of what we do at Eucharist and how the Eucharist transforms us to become more fully who we are called to be in our everyday life. Celebrating Eucharist is all about remembering our relationship with Jesus, a relationship that is always with us. The remembering, though, is not just remembering in our head, like some thought or memory. No, it means to remember in such a powerful way that His presence, His relationship is actually experienced here and now, and we are so caught up in it that we are changed by it. Eucharist helps us to remember the truth of who we are as members of the body of Christ (and therefore as people who are supposed to live and behave in a certain way), so that we don't suffer from spiritual amnesia and forget what is most important—our relationship with Jesus Christ. It's that relationship that makes us who we are. The fact that He is always with us—walking our journey with us and sharing His life with us—is the truth of our identity as Christians, and we are lost and in trouble when we forget that. We are truly who we are when we remember our intimate connection to Jesus and to one another because we are called to be His body. That's the truth of who we are, and nowhere is that expressed more fully or more powerfully than when the Church gathers to celebrate the Eucharist.

This was certainly true for the early Church. They gathered for the "breaking of the bread" and the "sharing of the cup." They assembled because they needed to participate in the activity that would cause them to recognize His presence. The people were there not just to listen to the prayers and to watch the priest do everything. There were no spectators at Eucharist in the early church because they brought their connected moments with them to remember their story; they were not there just to receive but to be transformed!

The first followers of Jesus knew Him, walked with Him, ate with Him, and shared their intimate thoughts with Him as they shared their hopes and dreams about God and God's kingdom. After knowing Jesus, they could never be the same again. After His death and resurrection, they had to remember Jesus and continue to experience His presence. They did this by doing what He did with them so often and especially what He did on the night before He died: they shared a meal together. In this meal, they were not just remembering Him, but He was actually there with them. Recall the story of the disciples on the Road to Emmaus in Luke's Gospel (24:13-35). What is the climax of that story? It's how they recognized, *in the breaking of the bread,* that Jesus was with them all along! In that recognition, they were transformed—they were changed by His presence.

That's the heart of the eucharistic action and the meaning of full participation at Mass: the action and participation of encountering the Lord, doing what He did, being changed by it and being formed by it to become what we are, namely, what the Eucharist is—His presence in the world, His Body, the life-giving gift of Jesus to the world. That's why we gather—not just to receive but to do what He did and be changed. We become Eucharist through the actions of experiencing, being changed, and then living that mystery of dying and rising every moment of every day. To live eucharistically is to live what we call the *Paschal Mystery*, the dying and rising of Jesus, as we give ourselves away (offer ourselves) in self-emptying love, finding our life by losing it. It means that because we are a priestly people, we live our life as a sacrifice—not sacrifice in the sense of destruction or killing, but sacrifice in the sense of offering one's life as a gift and being transformed by God. To live eucharistically is to live a life of offering, a life we unite with Jesus' offering in the celebration of Mass.

Bringing the offering of our life and joining it to the action of communal worship

We've all heard the excuse, I don't go to Mass because I don't get anything out of it. The fallacy of that statement is obvious; it's not a question of what we get out of it, it's a question of what we bring to it. What we must bring to it is a life lived eucharistically; what we must bring to it is the offering of ourselves. We must bring that offering and unite it to the communal action of the body, the offering of all the other members of the body of Christ with whom we are one. That unity in the body is the truth of who we are; we are not saved individually, but rather we are saved as members of a community.

At one point or another, each of us must ask ourselves the question, "Why do we come to Eucharist?" Do we think it makes a difference that we are there—and not just a difference to me, in terms of what I personally get out of it, but does it make a difference to the person next to me, to everyone else there, even to the people in the church who are strangers to me?

We hear in Luke's Gospel (4:14-21) how Jesus, while attending a synagogue service, was invited to do the reading. After the reading, He offered His explanation, His interpretation: "Today

this Scripture passage is fulfilled in your hearing." His interpretation was the message of the Good News: *He* would be the one
to bring glad tidings to the poor, liberty to captives, sight to the
blind. For Jesus, the message of God was not punishment, nor
wrath and doom, but the good news that He Himself was the
one to bring the Kingdom of God into our midst.

"Today, this Scripture passage is fulfilled in your hearing."
Perhaps that's the most important reason for us to gather at
Eucharist. Salvation is present in the person of Jesus whenever
we gather to read and preach the Sacred Scriptures and share
the eucharistic meal. It's something for us to think about: the
deepest, most profound, most personal way for anyone to discover God is when we come together with other people. If I
want to personally find out what God is saying to me and
doing for me, I can find it out— in its fullest sense—in a public
gathering. If I truly want to bring the offering of my life to the
Lord, I must do so by bringing it to the eucharistic assembly,
the gathering of the body of Christ. I must bring my life to the
community.

This does not negate the need for personal and private
prayer time. We should pray to God in the solitude of our heart
every day to nurture our relationship. The point, though, is that
private prayer is not enough; it's only half the picture. That
might sound like a strange thing to say, because, after all, if we
want to get in touch with God shouldn't we go off by ourselves
and pray? If something is so deeply personal, then doesn't that
mean it's individual? Not when it comes to liturgy. We need to
understand what it means to worship *as a body*. We don't celebrate liturgy as a group of individuals who happen to be in the
same place at the same time doing the same things; instead, we
pray together as one. As Catholics, our prayer life is incomplete
and our relationship with God is lacking if it does not include

participating in the communal act of worship that is the celebration of the Eucharist, praying not as individuals who happen to be together, but rather praying as one body.

I think the following example is relevant. Before I went into the seminary, I was studying to be an elementary school teacher. I remember learning in one of my child development courses about the concept of parallel play. Parallel play is a phenomenon that occurs with young children around the ages of 2 and 3. Children that age may be in close proximity to each other, perhaps sitting on the floor, and it may appear as though they are playing together. One might observe behaviors such as one child putting down a toy and the other child picking up that toy. It may look like they are interacting, but child development experts tell us actually they are not because at that stage of development children are still too egocentric to really relate to each other; they are still too much in their own little worlds. Consequently, even though the two children are sitting facing each other, they are not really interacting, but rather they are playing parallel to each other.

Using the phenomenon of parallel play as an example, I wonder how often we at worship actually *parallel pray*. In other words, I fear that the members of the liturgical assembly, rather than really praying together as a body, might instead be praying individually alongside others in a parallel way. The liturgical action calls for a unity deeper than that, however. Is our participation in worship sometimes like that of library patrons who sit at study carrels side-by-side, each person focused in his or her own world even though they are present at the same time in the library? It shouldn't be like that when we are at liturgy. Liturgical celebrations call us to get out of our own little world and enter into the actions of the community worshipping together.

Living eucharistically means accepting the challenge to understand that the most personal is not the most individual, at least not when it comes to faith. If we are wondering, *How can I find out who God is? How can I find out what God means to me? How can I live out my faith?*, then God is calling us to answer those questions not in isolation but in the midst of a community—the community that is the body of Christ at worship. Can we believe that one of the most profound reasons we celebrate Eucharist is ultimately because it is the best setting, the best context for us to discover God? Our faith never rests ultimately in "God-and-me;" ultimately, faith is about "God-and-us." Only by gathering at the Eucharist and entering into the act of worship not as an individual with others, but as a member of a body radically connected to others, can we understand the fullness of how faith applies to life. Only by bringing the offering of my life to the celebration of the Eucharist in union with the other members of the body can we make the proper connection that will allow us to live our entire life eucharistically in all its fullness.

The four actions we do as a community

There are four central actions that we do as the body of Christ when we ritually enact the celebration of the Eucharist. To live life eucharistically means that we connect these four basic actions in the celebration of the Eucharist with the ways we live those actions in our everyday life. The four actions I am speaking about are probably familiar to you. You have heard or read them every time you have heard or read the stories of the feeding miracles in the Scriptures, where Jesus feeds four or five thousand people. You have heard them or read them every time you have heard or read the accounts of the Last Supper. They are the actions described in the story of the disciples on the road to Emmaus mentioned earlier. Those Scripture stories tell us how Jesus performed these four actions on those occasions. Of course, you have most certainly heard them every time you have participated in the celebration of Mass when the priest proclaims them in the Eucharistic Prayer.

The actions are: Jesus *took* bread, *blessed* it, *broke* it, and *gave* it. Taking, blessing, breaking, and giving: these are the actions of celebrating the Eucharist, and these are the actions that help us to live the spirituality of the Eucharist. We must recognize Him in those actions at Mass, and we must allow those actions to become the rhythm, the heartbeat, and the lifeblood of our life so we can make the connection that that's who we are: people who take, bless, break, and give both at Mass and in our everyday life, because *The Body of Christ . . . I am/we are.* That's the truth of who we are and who we are to become. It's what makes you, you; me, me; and us, us.

Permit me a disclaimer at this point. As I said earlier, this book is not intended as a comprehensive treatise on eucharistic theology. Instead, I have chosen to focus on spiritual reflections based on the four actions of taking, blessing, breaking, and giving, the actions of the second half of the Mass, the Liturgy of the Eucharist. Admittedly, there is much that could be said about the Liturgy of the Word: e.g., our full, conscious, and active participation in the readings; how Christ is present in the Word; and how the Liturgy of the Word and the Liturgy of the Eucharist form one act of worship. A lack of discussion about this first part of the Mass should not be taken to mean I think it is unimportant, or not integral, or as though it were just a prelude to the "real part" of the Mass. This is simply the result of my choice to focus directly on taking, blessing, breaking, and giving.

Let's now take a look at those four eucharistic actions and see how we can connect those ritual actions at Mass with our everyday life so that we might truly *live* eucharistically.

TAKING

Connecting Everyday Life with the Presentation of the Gifts

THE taking action, first among the four-fold sequence of actions of taking, blessing, breaking, and giving occurs at the Presentation of the Gifts. It is here that the gifts of bread and wine (and often money) are brought forward to the priest to be placed on the altar. This is much more than just a functional carrying up of the gifts; it is not meant to be a practical, lifeless moving of the bread and wine to the altar. Instead, this procession with the gifts of bread and wine that will be transformed into the Body and Blood of Christ is an important moment meant to be a key expression of our full, conscious, and active participation in the celebration of the Eucharist.

Those gifts of bread and wine are meant to symbolize us— they represent the gift of ourselves. The central action of Mass is that everyone who is present unites the offering of their life to the offering of Christ, as everything is lifted up to the Father in union with his Son Jesus: "through Him, and with Him, and in Him." It is the sacrifice of our life that is placed on the altar with the gifts of bread and wine. The sacrifice acceptable to God, however, is a life lived in love and self-emptying. Without truly living the life of love that Jesus commands us to live, our worship at Mass is nothing more than empty ritual, a meaningless observance devoid of content. If we don't bring the gift of ourselves and surrender ourselves to God, then we are simply engaging in an external observance. In other words, we must hand everything over to God, placing everything we have and are on the altar so that God might accept it and transform it for His purpose and His glory, as surely as He will transform the bread and the wine into the Body and Blood of Christ.

In essence, then, the spirituality of the taking action involves the spirituality of holding nothing back from God; it means being willing to bring every aspect of one's life and lay it bare before God in total trust and dependency. This includes everything that we have lived and everything we have experienced since the last time we celebrated Mass. Certainly we should bring the good things we have done: the ways we have been loving, the ways we have lived the life of Christ, the ways we have been the presence of Jesus for others. We should bring them and give them back to God, since we cannot do good things on our own; such goodness is itself a gift from God, having its origin in Him. We can praise God by placing on the altar the bread and wine of the love we have lived, knowing that such love nourished and gave life to others as spiritual food in the same way that bread and wine nourish us.

We can also bring the parts of our life that aren't so pretty and aren't so perfect; we can bring our sinfulness, since we need God to forgive our sin, heal us of our evil, and transform us and make us new. We can bring everything that needs to be lifted up to God because it needs to be made new: we can bring our child who is ill with cancer or some other life-threatening disease; we can bring our own illnesses and addictions; we can bring our hopes and our search for meaning; we can bring our anger and our hatred. We should bring anything and everything that we need and want to be touched and made new by God: our thankfulness and our praise, the good we have done and the good we want to do but have failed to do. We take it all and place it on the altar and through the prayers and actions of the Mass, we say, "Take it, God, and make it part of You. Accept my offering—the offering of myself—so that You might transform it to make it, and me, more into the image and likeness of Jesus."

Interestingly, this is why the money taken up during the collection is often presented along with the gifts of bread and wine. In the ancient Church, people would actually bring their own offerings of bread, wine, and other foods; the procession with gifts would be a moment when all brought their gifts forward. Bread and wine needed for the celebration of the Eucharist would be used for that purpose, and the remainder would be set aside for distribution to the poor. Thus a very direct connection would be made between liturgy and life, between Mass and everyday living. To live in the image and likeness of Jesus means to offer yourself not only to God the Father, but also to your brothers and sisters in need. Although other token symbolic gifts should not be brought up to the altar and presented at this time of the Mass (e.g., school projects, secular objects, etc.), but rather only the gifts of bread and wine that will be transformed, it is possible to also bring forward the collection of money as the modern-day equivalent of the offering of oneself in charity to those in need. In addition, insofar as money symbolizes one's offering to the poor, it is also acceptable for actual gifts for the poor, such as food items, to be brought forward. The U. S. bishops have commented on this:

> In addition to money, gifts in kind and other real gifts for the poor are appropriate, but not token items that will be retrieved and returned to ordinary use after the celebration.[6]

---

[6] United States Conference of Catholic Bishops, *Introduction to the Order of Mass: A Pastoral Resource of the Bishops' Committee on the Liturgy,* Pastoral Liturgy Series 1 (Washington D.C., 2003), #105, p. 79.

All of this presumes, of course, that we come to Mass ready to bring the gift of ourselves. We must be conscious and aware of the spirituality of this action of taking and its connection to our everyday life. If, in fact, we feel that our celebration of Mass is not as fulfilling as it should be, it might be because we are not making these connections. Perhaps the problem is not that we are doing a poor job at liturgy; perhaps the problem is that we are doing a poor job at Christian living! Maybe the key to effective "taking" at Mass is to really see how every moment of every day in every part of life can be an occasion to offer ourselves to God as we see His presence and His invitation to live the life of Jesus more closely by offering ourselves to others.

The gifts of bread and wine should be the common symbols of everyone at Mass. Just as the token items in *The Wizard of Oz* were the symbols, or triggers, of what had been with the characters all along, so too should the bread and wine at Mass trigger or symbolize for us the connection with the daily life that we are living in Christ. Let's reflect more on this connection.

The presence of God in ordinary moments

In the eighth grade I participated in a Vocational Interest Survey to determine my educational and career interests. I always find it interesting to look back at the results.

According to the way I answered the questions, my number one choice of occupation was Teaching, Counseling, and Social Work. The description for this category read: "providing instruction or other services in a school, college, church, clinic, or welfare agency." My second choice was calculated to be Literary, which meant "writing novels, poetry, reviews, speeches, or technical reports; editing; translating."

Now, you'll have to believe me when I say that at age 13 I had absolutely no idea whatsoever about becoming a priest.

(Actually, had you asked me then, I would have told you I wanted to be a game show host!) The survey simply revealed my interest or aptitude, at that time, for the more ordinary, everyday, secular aspects of those occupations.

I do find it interesting that my chosen vocation—priesthood—combines many of my interests and gifts in a way that perhaps no other profession or vocation could. More so, as I look back on my life, I realize this was not an isolated incident. There were many occasions, tendencies, and personal choices that, although ordinary and commonplace in and of themselves, came together in such a way that I eventually realized that for me, priesthood was the vocation that would bring it all together in the best way possible. And so eventually I made a free choice (and continue to make that choice) to accept that God was (and is still!) calling me to priesthood.

Another way of saying this is that grace—the action of God in our life—is often a strange combination of both the gifts we have been given from God and how we choose to use them. It's that strange combination of the "ordinary" and the "grace-filled" that we should take to the altar in every celebration of the Eucharist.

The fact is that many events in our life seem to have an "ordinary" face stamped on them, a "secular" image, an everyday inscription. Do we really believe, however, that it is the "secular" that is the normal setting for the spiritual to work in—that the ordinary bread and wine of our life become the vehicles for God's transformative power, just as occurs with the eucharistic bread and wine? Do we realize that the face of God, the sign of His sovereignty, is stamped on all of the events of our life? Do we recognize that it is God's life and love that make the "ordinary" situation possible in the first place? Grace is written into the very fabric of "nature," since nature cannot exist without grace in the first place!

Can we recognize the moments of our life where grace is present? In the Eucharist, the ordinariness of bread and wine is used as a vehicle for expressing the presence of the Risen Christ among us, as we are asked to take the ordinariness of our life and bring it to the altar as a vehicle for the holy.

Our creatureliness

Certainly a large part of the ordinariness of our life is that we are human and finite. Unfortunately, we often think of creatureliness, limitedness, finitude, temptation, as something negative; we mistakenly think that if only we could escape it, then things would be wonderful. We imagine how great it would be if only we could get away from the muck and mire of being human and sinful and rise out of the muddiness of life. Yet, it is exactly this limited, human, finite, sinful, and wounded life that God wants us to bring as our offering so that He can touch it, transform it, and give it back to us renewed.

Bread and wine, fruit of the earth, and vine and work of human hands, remind us that humanity, creatureliness, finitude, and temptation are not something to escape, but rather are exactly the things we cannot live without because they are the very avenues for growth in God, the very structures for encountering new life, the very elements which God will transform. How amazing it is that God allows us to offer ourselves as we are, not waiting (thank goodness!) for when we are all prettied up. Being able to take the bread and wine of our lives as they are here and now—not waiting until they are as we would like them to be, but as they are now—is a wonderful gift from God. He is telling us that it is in the midst of our limitedness and finitude that He works His most wondrous ways—

even in the parts of our life we think may not be all that conducive to grace.

For example, let's look at temptation, something that at first glance we might think is a negative part of the spiritual life and therefore has no place at the altar. The truth is that when we are tempted, it can actually be a positive thing because it can be an opportunity for growth and grace. Temptation presents us with a moment of choice, to follow what is truthful and what will lead to greater goodness or to follow a lie. If we are struggling with a temptation in our life, it is exactly that temptation that we should take to the altar to be touched, and healed, and transformed by God.

Indeed, the moments when we are tempted—when, you might say, we are capable of the greatest sin—those are also the moments when we are most open to grace. Those are exactly the moments that need to be taken to the altar!

Adam and Eve sinned not because they were tempted, but because they chose to follow a lie. When we hear about "the tree of the knowledge of good and evil" in the book of Genesis, scholars tell us we are hearing a phrase that expresses a totality of experience that is inappropriate to human creatureliness. God created us to be limited, finite—in other words, human—and God said that was *good*. But, Adam and Eve chose to believe the lie that being human wasn't good enough, and that they knew better than God. Thus, when Adam and Eve eat the fruit of the tree, they are attempting to attain a mastery over their lives and an autonomy apart from God that is inappropriate for a creature created by God. They sinned by rejecting what God created them to be.

If God is telling us it is the bread and wine of our lives, and all of our life—the good, the bad, and the ugly—that we should hand over to Him, then who are we to say that it's not good enough for God? Don't we believe that God can accept it and transform it? Don't we want to experience the new, resurrected life that God will bring about?

Sacramental living: there's a goodness to life that we recognize now

Taking the bread and wine of our life as it is here and now helps us to have an appropriate Christian optimism about life on earth.

"There must be a heaven, because life on earth is hell." Have you ever heard that saying, or perhaps said something similar yourself? Sometimes that feeling is expressed in anger and frustration by someone deeply wounded by life circumstances. Some people even use this attitude as an excuse to cop out of practicing their faith; they say, "How can I go to church and believe in God when I see so much suffering and evil in the world here and now?"

Sadly, that attitude is not very Christian, and certainly not eucharistic. A Christian has the attitude that is expressed in Romans 8:35, 37-39: "Who can separate us from the love of Christ? Will hardship, or distress, or persecution, or famine or nakedness, or danger, or the sword? . . . No, throughout all these things we are conquerors because of him who loved us. For I am convinced that neither death, nor life, nor angels, nor principalities, nor present things, nor things to come, nor powers, nor height, nor depth, nor any othere creature will be able to separate us from the love of God in Christ Jesus our Lord." To live eucharistically demands that we have the confidence, the outlook, and the vision that proclaims to the world, "Yes, God is here and will not abandon us."

Celebrating the Eucharist challenges us to have that confidence and that vision. Every time we celebrate the Eucharist we are challenged to be people who have a Catholic perception of reality.

"A Catholic perception of reality" means having a sacramental view of life. One of the best things about our Catholic heritage is our sacramental tradition: our understanding of the power of sacraments and our whole sacramental view of reality. A good way to think of a sacrament is as a pointer: a sacrament points to, highlights, or makes visible what is already there, but which is in some way hidden. Once revealed, it has a powerful, transformative effect in our life. As children we learned that the Church has seven official sacraments, but there are also many other "sacraments" in the world and in life because many other things can reveal God's presence in our midst and become occasions for conversion and transformation.

This is true because as Catholics we believe that God's love, God's power, God's grace (all different ways of saying the same thing) are in abundance. God loves us with an overabundance from which we cannot be separated and which exceeds anything we could expect or imagine.

To have a Catholic sacramental vision of life, then, is to believe in this abundance and to believe we can see it, experience it, taste it here and now because certain things point it out for us. Catholics are the ones who say, "Look at that ocean, or mountain, or sunset, or other person, or act of love; *that* points to God." In a world that hungers to see God, in a world that clings to empty, temporary fulfillments that really don't satisfy, in a world that cries out, "How do you find God? How do you know God is there? What does God look like?" Catholics are the ones right there with the answer, "God is right in front of your eyes; this is pointing to God, and that is too, if only you will make the effort to look." We see God's presence in the ordinary bread and wine of everyday life.

Seeing aspects of the bread and wine of our everyday life as occasions for God's presence, and then connecting them to the bread and wine taken to the altar, is easy once we are conscious of making the connections. For example, the real, exclusive, and intimate love between a husband and wife is a sign of the way God intimately loves each of us. Our care for the sick is God's way of caring for the sick. Our willingness to forgive each other gives us an insight into God's super-abundant forgiveness. Our efforts to help the poor show God's concern for the poor. A sacramental vision tells us that God's goodness and love are all around us in abundance, but we can only see it in the bread and wine (which earth has given and human hands have made) of our ordinary, human, self-giving love for one another, not in possessions, power, or selfishness. If we can make this connection, God will never again seem absent; instead, we will see how inseparable God really is from us. It becomes easy to take the bread and wine of our life to the altar since it is obviously all around us.

Taking what we have NOW

Another important aspect of the taking action is to trust enough to bring our life to God as it is NOW. We all have an image of how we would like our life to be—free of all sins, faults, and suffering. Wouldn't it be great if our life was a steady, uphill progression toward holiness? In that kind of ideal existence, we would always know what God wants, and we would always do it perfectly.

Our life is not like that, though, is it? That's not reality, and that's okay. Holiness is being able to see when we have failed and need to start over again. Holiness is about having the trust and freedom to turn back to God. Holiness is about being able to experience God's love so much that we are willing to take the bread and wine of our life as it is—here and now—and place it on the altar.

After all, Jesus' central proclamation of the Kingdom of God was the proclamation of forgiveness. An essential part of that forgiveness is that in God's mercy for sinners, something new is always possible; there is always the NOW of a new beginning with God.

In the Gospel of Matthew, chapter 21, verses 28-32, Jesus tells the parable about the two sons, one of whom refuses the father's command to go work in the vineyard, but who then later changes his mind and does as the father wanted, and the other son who says yes immediately but winds up never going. In the setting in which Matthew gives us this parable, the chief priests and elders to whom Jesus addressed the story had the same opportunity as the tax collectors and prostitutes to hear the truth, to see the error of their ways and to repent, but they refused to take advantage of the opportunities God offered them "now" in Jesus.

So, if your life is not a steady, straight, uphill climb to holiness, that's no problem for God. If we make a wrong choice, that sin need not label us forever. We can always be converted if we allow ourselves to be converted, since God always offers us new life—God is always now. A person can never be totally summed up in one action, one word, one thought, or one sin. We must never foreclose on ourselves or on others, since God does not judge by the past.

You had an abortion? That need not define you for the rest of your life; God is offering you an invitation now. You betrayed someone or hurt someone? You need not carry the past around anymore; God is offering you a chance to heal and be reconciled with that person. Whatever the sin, or whatever the darkness or brokenness of our past, it pales in comparison to the possibility for the future God wants to make for us if we will simply bring it to Him! None of these need be excluded from being taken to the altar in order to be healed and transformed by God.

At every Mass, after the gifts of bread and wine have been taken to the altar and have been prepared by being prayed over, the priest says, "Pray, brothers and sisters, that my sacrifice and *yours* may be acceptable to God, the almighty Father." That's an incredible "now opportunity" to bring to God the gift, the sacrifice of our life as it is at this very moment. Regardless of what that "now" might look like, it's an invitation to try to let go of the past and to change. God does not say, "Bring yourself to me when you are perfect." God does not say, "Bring yourself to me when you have finished the climb to holiness." God does say, "Bring yourself now, as you are, and I will make you something new."

Zacchaeus as a good example

Remember the story of Zacchaeus in Luke's Gospel?

Jesus entered Jericho and was passing through it. A man there, named Zacchaeus, was a chief tax collector and a rich man. He wanted to see who Jesus was, but since he was short in stature, he could not see him because of the crowd. Therefore, he ran ahead and climbed a sycamore tree in order to catch a glimpse of him for he was going to pass that way.

When he reached that spot, Jesus looked up and said to him, "Zacchaeus, hurry and come down, for I must stay at your house today." Zacchaeus came down quickly and welcomed him joyfully.

When the people observed this, they began to complain, saying, "He has gone to be the guest of a man who is a sinner." But Zacchaeus stood there and said to the Lord, "Behold, Lord, I intend to give half of everything I possess to the poor, and if I have defrauded someone of anything, I will repay that amount four times over."

Then Jesus said to him, "Today salvation has come to this house, because this man too is a son of Abraham. For the Son of Man has come to seek out and to save what was lost." (Lk 19:1-10)

It was actually quite an absurd thing for Zacchaeus to do. Zacchaeus literally went out on a limb—climbed a tree—in order to see Jesus. This probably looked kind of silly to everyone watching him, and it was dangerous, too. But it was also risky and dangerous in another sense.

Consider Zacchaeus' status in the community: everyone knew who he was because they all hated him! He was despised by the people because he was a chief tax collector and a wealthy man. That meant he was a Jew who allied himself with the Romans, the occupying government. In essence, Zacchaeus was a traitor, collecting money for the enemy. On top of that, Zacchaeus was dishonest: he collected more than was necessary and kept the profit for himself.

So, it probably was not a very good idea for him to draw such attention to himself in the midst of a crowd. Yet, it was this very act that got him noticed by the Lord; it was only because Zacchaeus literally went out on a limb that he was in a position to hear Jesus say, "Today I must stay at your house." Conversion always starts because of the Lord's initiative. Jesus always makes the first move to save us; we do not save ourselves. However, we must be sure that we are in a position to be able to hear the Lord's invitation; we must be ready and able to respond to His call as He leads us to grace and new life.

Perhaps we can think of taking the bread and wine of our life to the altar as a kind of "going out on a limb" in order to be able to hear and respond to Jesus. Jesus sought Zacchaeus out and, when he found him, Zacchaeus was converted; he changed; he found salvation. Could it be, then, that conversion begins by "going out on a limb?" In other words, if we want to change our life—to be free of something bad so that we can finally turn toward something new—then perhaps we too have to go out on a limb and do something that might seem a little absurd in some way in order to begin to respond to the conversion process initiated by Jesus' invitation.

Being converted and coming closer to God does not just happen on its own, just as moving away from God and into sin doesn't just happen. Many times a sinful pattern is the result of small choices we have made along the way, decisions that have built up over time to lead us down the road to where we are now.

Conversion, then, means changing by starting with the ordinary bread and wine of small, daily decisions that will begin to bring us back to God. The little decisions to take our life to God, as symbolized by a connection with the taking of the bread and wine to the altar at Mass, can be the start of this. Conversion means breaking patterns by making small decisions that may seem silly or even absurd, but, in fact, actually help us on our way in the long run. For example, in preparing for a marathon, a runner does not start out by running 26 miles. Instead, the runner builds up to the full distance by running small distances, and then gradually running longer and longer increments until his or her body is trained to endure the long haul. So, too, when we are trying to make a behavioral change in our life that will benefit us spiritually. If, for example, we find ourselves attracted to pornography, simply thinking "I don't want to do that anymore" may not be enough. We may need to make lots of small decisions, such as planning steps to avoid boredom, or organizing our time to avoid the loneliness that leads to going to inappropriate websites, so that we can build up the virtuous dispositions and habits that will eventually lead to the real change in the long run.

Like Zacchaeus, salvation comes to us and to our house when we take the risk and the steps to respond to the goodness that God sees in us, and when we do our part to bring out that goodness more clearly by changing our life in some small way here and now. God begins to transform us as soon as we take ourselves to Him to be converted, no matter how small or absurd that step might be. Taking ourselves to Him along with the bread and wine can be the symbol of how we will take ourselves to Him once we leave Mass, so that we can begin the road of conversion, healing, forgiveness, and new life.

The next time you are celebrating the Eucharist, go out on a limb and ask yourself, *How do I need to be saved? What part of my life still needs to be converted more perfectly to Jesus? Where do I need to change in order to be reconciled with God and with others?*

What is it that you have to do, no matter how small, or silly, or absurd it might look, in order to open yourself to the salvation that Jesus wants to bring—and that only Jesus can bring—to your house? Discover that, and take that to the altar with the bread and wine.

Making connections

The taking action of the Mass then is all about making the connections between our faith and our everyday life. The things we said and did, the virtues and the sins, the people we treated with dignity and the people we dismissed with rudeness, the times we trusted in God and the times we despaired, are all bread and wine that need to be taken to the altar.

Now when we hear someone say, "Mass is boring, I don't get anything out of it," hopefully we understand that it is not what we get out of it, but what we bring to it that matters! We must bring all the relationships, events, hopes, and fears that make up our ordinary, everyday life and we must hand them over to God, lifting them up: "Lift up your hearts / We lift them up to the Lord." Then, lifting up our hearts with the bread and wine, we too will be transformed to be more like Him. Our love will become God's love; our compassion will be God's compassion; our forgiveness will be God's forgiveness; our mercy will be God's mercy.

3

BLESSING

Connecting Everyday Life with the Eucharistic Prayer

W E now turn to the action of blessing, an action that includes the consecration of the bread and wine into the Body and Blood of Christ, and also encompasses a richness and a depth beyond that one action. To be sure, consecration takes place, and through the prayer of the Church and the power of the Holy Spirit bread and wine are transformed into the Real Presence of the Body and Blood of Christ. However, it's in that very notion of "transformation" that the consecration is brought into the wider meaning of blessing. This is where we need to understand the Eucharistic Prayer in its entirety. We need to enter into the fullness of the Eucharistic Prayer in its various parts, understanding the entire prayer to be a prayer of blessing and consecration, not just one part of it. The *General Instruction of the Roman Missal* says this about the Eucharistic Prayer in paragraph 78:

Now the center and summit of the entire celebration begins: namely, the Eucharistic Prayer, that is, the prayer of thanksgiving and sanctification. The priest invites the people to lift up their hearts to the Lord in prayer and thanksgiving; he unites the congregation with himself in the prayer that he addresses in the name of the entire community to God the Father through Jesus Christ in the Holy Spirit. Furthermore, **the meaning of the Prayer is that the entire congregation of the faithful should join**

itself with Christ in confessing the great deeds of God and in the offering of Sacrifice.[7] (emphasis added)

It's clear, then, that everyone, according to his or her role in the liturgical assembly, joins in the blessing action insofar as everyone joins in "confessing the great deeds of God and in the offering of Sacrifice." The priest, as presider and acting in the person of Christ the Head, has his unique and irreplaceable role to play in proclaiming the Eucharistic Prayer. Yet, everyone present participates in the prayer through the uniting of their sacrifice to Christ and in offering the sacrifice of the Church.

Because a key part of eucharistic praying is the lifting up of one's heart to the Lord and joining oneself to Christ, we might say that to bless is to unite the divine and the human; this is what links the blessing action to the taking action that came before it. In the prayer of blessing that is the Eucharistic Prayer, we ask God to accept what we offer and to redeem it, to transform it, and to make it a part of Himself. When the human is united with the divine, the human is transformed.

In the part of the Eucharistic Prayer called the *epiclesis*, the priest extends his hands over the gifts of bread and wine and prays for the Holy Spirit to come upon them to transform them into the Body and Blood of the Lord. The important thing for us to remember is that there is a "part two," so to speak, of that consecratory *epiclesis*. Later in the Eucharistic Prayer (after the Memorial Acclamation), the priest will pray again for the Holy Spirit to be an agent of transformation, this time upon us, the people. This second *epiclesis* is referred to as a communion *epiclesis*, since the transformation that is invoked is a transformation of being brought together into unity.

---

[7] Liturgy Documentary Series 2, United States Conference of Catholic Bishops (Washington D.C., 2003).

When the Holy Spirit comes down upon something, transformation occurs. One aspect of that transformation is that unity is brought about: union between the divine and the human, in addition to unity among all those who share in the gift of the Eucharist. Within the Eucharistic Prayer, the transformation occurs against the larger backdrop of memorial, or *anamnesis*. Recall, if you will, the quotation from paragraph 79 of the *General Instruction of the Roman Missal* mentioned in chapter one: the action of praying eucharistically involves remembering, then offering ("we remember, therefore we offer"). In that action, transformation occurs. As the Church remembers the saving acts of God—specifically, the Paschal Mystery, the saving death and resurrection of the Lord Jesus—the saving power of that mystery is again made present and we are caught up in it; that's why we are challenged to unite the offering of our life to Jesus' offering, made effectively present. It is in the action of remembering-offering-being transformed (which should be seen as one action, not three) that heaven and earth meet in the liturgy; it is in that action that the divine and the human are brought together. Participation in the celebration of the Eucharist means being swept up into that meeting of the divine and the human. Living eucharistically means to live and pray in such a way that the action of praying eucharistically as proclaimed in the Eucharistic Prayer (remembering-offering-being transformed) becomes the very rhythm and focus of one's life every moment of every day.

The key is identification with Christ

Insofar as the Eucharistic Prayer memorializes and makes present the saving power of the Paschal Mystery—Christ's passage through death into new life—then the challenge is to identify ourselves with that passage not only in the celebration of Mass, but in the liturgy that is our life. The key is to live life in such a way that one's identification with Christ in every situation is indeed a kind of "Eucharistic prayer of memorial and blessing," because the saving power of Christ's Paschal Mystery is being recalled and is effective in the very situation one is facing.

I share with you a very powerful example of this kind of identification with Christ in the story of my friends Tony and Kathy. Tony and I have been friends since high school, and Tony and Kathy actually set their wedding date around my ordination date so that I could preside at their Nuptial Mass and receive their vows as a priest. They were married exactly one week after I was ordained. Their beautiful marriage was blessed with three lovely children. While those three children were still young, however, Kathy was stricken with cancer. It was a humbling experience for me to be a part of the journey of this faith-filled couple as they battled the disease and as they continued to turn to their faith for strength and support.

On one occasion Kathy confided to me that she had just gone for a rather crucial test that would give a great deal of information about her prognosis. She told me that because of where her cancer was, she had to undergo the exam with her arms stretched out, and that in the midst of the test it suddenly occurred to her that she was just like Jesus on the cross with His arms outstretched. Somehow that thought gave her great comfort in facing whatever the future would bring.

Some time later, at a time when it was obvious that nothing more could be done and that the cancer would take her life, Kathy shared with me an even more profound identification with Christ. Her exact words to me were: "I don't know why I have to go through this, Joe, but I do. But Jesus had to go through this too. So somehow, I know that Tony and the kids are going to be alright."

Truly, that is the identification with Jesus that allows one to live life eucharistically! Kathy remembered the Paschal Mystery, Jesus' passage through death into new life, and found hope for the future in that. She united herself to it and handed herself over to it and in so doing was transformed. This is the full meaning of blessing in the sense of uniting the divine and the human. Being swept up into the saving mystery of Jesus is the dynamic that is at work in the entire Eucharistic Prayer, a prayer of blessing.

The entire Eucharistic Prayer

Every Catholic should have the Eucharistic Prayer as the center of his or her spirituality. Have you ever spent time slowly and meditatively reflecting on the words of the different Eucharistic Prayers? If not, I urge you to do so. Find the texts in a prayer book, or in a missalette, or on the internet, and spend time with them. Perhaps they could be the focus of a retreat you make. Pray over the prayer in its entirety and delve deeply into what the prayers are saying. Notice how the prayers recall the saving mystery of Jesus' death and resurrection. Notice how the prayers are prayed by the priest in the first person plural, "we," indicating how everyone is joined in praying the prayer. Locate in each prayer the action of "we remember, therefore we offer" and reflect on the rich spiritual meaning of that.

Think about how the words of consecration can be understood as something more than what happens only to the bread and wine. "Take this, all of you, and eat of it: for this is my body which will be given up for you." "Take this, all of you, and drink from it: for this is the chalice of my blood, the blood of the new and eternal covenant, which will be poured out for you and for many for the forgiveness of sins. Do this in memory of me."

We need to understand the words of consecration within the context of the entire Eucharistic Prayer, and therefore as words that refer not only to the "objects" of bread and wine, but also to the whole activity. Notice how the consecration of the elements is linked to activity: the bread becomes the Body *which will be given up*; the blood is His blood *which will be poured out for the forgiveness of sins*. The Lord's Real Presence in the Eucharist is never simply a "static presence" of "being there," but is always a dynamic, communicative presence where He is giving Himself to us for our transformation. Christ is present not simply to *be* but to *give*. Consequently, we who will receive those transformed gifts are not there simply to receive, but to die and to rise with Jesus as we give ourselves to Him and to others in self-giving love. That is the body of Christ: a body that always gives itself away. That is the truth of who we are as the body of Christ; that is what we are to be continually transformed into: those who make a radical identification with Christ. That is how we are to live eucharistically.

Let's reflect on some further aspects of the transformation that occurs in this action of blessing, and how it can impact the way we live a eucharistic life.

Transformation as a whole new way of looking at things

It's no secret to my family and friends that Olivia Newton-John is my favorite singer, and that I have long followed her career and her life story. Olivia was diagnosed with breast cancer on July 3, 1992. During her recovery from surgery, and as she was undergoing chemotherapy, she wrote a very personal collection of songs under the title of *Gaia*. One of the songs in

that collection is titled "Why Me," with some of the lyrics
being:

> Don't ask why me, why me why not me
> Why not me is the thing
> Life does the strangest things
> You never know what each moment can bring
> You turn around, your life has changed
> Every obstacle before you is a tool to face your fears
> Oh don't say why me

For me, those lyrics signal the grace of a transformation of a
whole new way of looking at things. Many times when we are
faced with adversity or suffering, the first question we ask is,
"Why me?" with the subtle implication being that somehow
God "did this to me" as though I were a target. Yet, true
eucharistic living helps us to realize that "Why me?" is the
wrong question to ask. Insofar as the celebration of the
Eucharist recalls the Paschal Mystery of Christ's suffering,
death, and resurrection, we remember that Christ Himself, the
Son of God, suffered and died by freely going to the cross. If
Jesus Himself willingly embraced the cross with confidence
and trust in His Father, can we do any less? The blessing of
eucharistic transformation helps us to shift the focus from ourselves to God and can help us believe in God's power to raise
us up in ways that we cannot even begin to imagine. God
raised His Son from the dead; God turned the utter powerless-
ness of Jesus' dead body into the glorified, risen body of our
triumphant King. He can do, and indeed does, the same for us.
We need to remember that as we bring the offering of ourselves
in trust and confidence—especially when that offering is some
cross or obstacle that we encounter as part of living the
eucharistic life.

Transformed into waiting and openness

Living eucharistically means being able to wait and be open. This kind of transformation is another grace that can come through our communal praying of the Eucharistic Prayer. As noted earlier, both the priest and the people pray the Eucharistic Prayer, though not in exactly the same way. The people have some things to sing (say) out loud: the responses to the dialogue at the beginning; the Holy, Holy; the Memorial Acclamation; and, most importantly, the Great Amen. For most of the Eucharistic Prayer, however, the priest is articulating the words out loud by himself. This does not mean that the people should be passive or just be spectators. Through their full attention and focus, they should be engaged in the prayer and joining their offering to Christ's, as we have already discussed. Just because the people are not "doing something" (i.e., speaking out loud, singing, or moving) during the prayer does not mean they are doing nothing. Most importantly, the members of the liturgical assembly can participate in the prayer by opening their hearts to God's transformative power.

This might be something that is difficult to do, especially given the nature of our modern-day culture. We live in a culture that constantly sends the message, "Do more; be active." Living eucharistically, however, calls us to remember that significant things can happen when we pause long enough to allow ourselves simply to be open to the transformative power of God.

Our attentive participation during the Eucharistic Prayer, (or, for that matter, during any part of the Mass) when we are not outwardly saying or "doing" anything, is a good example of how we are, in reality, truly "doing" something, namely, the work of full, conscious, and active participation. On one level we may seem to be doing nothing, but on a deeper level—the level of the Spirit—there's a great deal going on, in a way that we can't fully fathom, because we are letting God do something. Something unexplainable happens when we hand ourselves over to God, when we let go to a process grounded in the Holy Spirit, and when we just simply open ourselves to *becoming what God is transforming us into.* The challenge is to truly open ourselves up to this deeper level, the level on which we focus on our life not on a superficial level, but on the deeper level of who we are becoming—when we shift from an egotistical focus on what we have accomplished in terms of worldly success to instead focus on what we are allowing God to accomplish in us in our soul.

This touches on the essence of what prayer really is. Prayer is more than just saying prayers. Rather, to pray is to make oneself open and aware of a relationship with God. Prayer is a discovery of a center in our life, a recognition of our longing for intimacy and communion with God.

The toughest thing about real prayer is letting God do it in us, rather than thinking that we do it. With that kind of openness, our attitude changes and true transformation occurs. After all, the point of prayer is not to change God's mind, as though God does not know something or needs to hear it from us, but rather to hear from Him—to change our mind and our attitude so we can understand what God is saying to us and where God is leading us.

Such is the transformation in the Holy Spirit. That kind of transformation, that kind of prayer, is truly a remarkable thing. How else to explain someone who, although confined to a hospital bed, critically ill and dying, nonetheless praises God for God's goodness and is filled with love, not with bitterness and grief? Remember, faith does not release us from our problems, but it does equip us for life and gives us a way to face it. But it ᴄᴀ   ᴌy do this when we live on the level of the Spirit, namely, when we are open to the transformative power that only God can accomplish.

That's why silence at Mass is so important, by the way. We're often uncomfortable with silence, but it's necessary for us if we are going to be open to the Spirit. There should be pauses for silence at Mass before the Penitential Rite, when we are invited to call to mind our sins; when the priest says, "Let us pray" before the Opening Prayer; after each of the readings; after the homily; and after the Communion Procession has ended. Do we take advantage of those opportunities for silence?

Such moments are far from passive moments. Those moments should be active moments of concentrated, deliberate, awe-filled attentive silence and stillness that open us up to the transformative power of God. Seeds of silence planted there can blossom elsewhere. The moments of communal silence in the liturgy, if we truly give ourselves over to them, can blossom in our life outside of liturgy. Amidst the turmoil of everyday life, we can return to that silent place that was cultivated at liturgy; there will be a center inside us that we can visit and from which we can hear the voice of God. It's a mutual relationship, though: in order to be silent at Mass, we need to practice being silent at home and in our everyday life; and, to be able to be silent at home and in our everyday life, we need to cultivate silence at the appropriate points in the liturgy. This connection between liturgy and life is a key factor in living eucharistically.

Transformed into trusting in the future

One of the transformative effects of eucharistic living is believing that no matter what we go through now, somehow, some way, God takes and shapes it to fit into our ultimate redemption—God makes it work toward new life. That is, after all, the essence of the Paschal Mystery that is celebrated in the Eucharist.

However, we do have to be careful about this. For example, it does not mean that God makes bad things happen to us in order to test us or to strengthen our faith. Also, we never want to say that suffering is God's will for us. Those are handy rationalizations, but they simply are not true; such explanations make God out to be cruel and arbitrary. God never sends suffering. But, to believe that God takes our sufferings and shapes them to fit His purpose: that's faith; that's obedience; that's trusting in God; that's living eucharistically.

Jesus Christ Himself had to struggle with that kind of obedience. The Letter to the Hebrews reminds us: "During his life on earth, he [Jesus] offered up prayer and entreaty, with loud cries and with tears, to the one who had the power to save him from death, and, winning a hearing by his reverence, he learnt obedience, Son though he was, through his sufferings" (5:7-9). When speaking about Christ offering up "prayer and entreaty with loud cries and tears," the author of the Letter to the Hebrews is referring to Jesus' agony in the Garden of Gethsemane, as He struggled with accepting the cross, asking the Father, if possible, to let the "cup" (of suffering) pass from Him. Jesus shared our human experience in all things but sin, and so He, too, wrestled with placing His trust totally in God when all things pointed against doing so. Jesus' anguish in the Garden is clearly portrayed in the Gospels. Yes, the Father answered Jesus' prayer, but not by saving Jesus from death. Instead, the Father brought Jesus through death to the resurrection. Through Jesus' death and resurrection, God brought Him "to perfection," i.e., to fulfillment. The anguish Jesus experienced in the present was shaped by God into a glorious future.

St. John explains it in his Gospel in terms of the grain of wheat which must fall to the ground and die (12:20-33). Remember that John's Gospel does not include Jesus' agony in the Garden of Gethsemane as the other three Gospels do, but in the passage about the grain of wheat Jesus explains the meaning of His death. The seed is buried in the ground and then bears fruit; Jesus, by dying, bears fruit: He gives life to others. Death is the means of gaining life; what seems like destruction now is shaped by God into life for the future.

Jesus' obedience—His trust that the sufferings of the present would be shaped by His Father into the glories of the future—is the model for all of us who follow Jesus and who are striving to live eucharistically, in the pattern of His Paschal Mystery. As disciples, we are invited to see His way, His journey, and His obedience as our way, our journey, and our obedience. Sharing in Jesus' risen life means sharing in the mystery that risen life is obtained only through death. To be obedient as Jesus was obedient means to trust that God will make it all fit together, despite our distress and pain.

Admittedly, this is difficult to accept, and it's natural for us to doubt this sometimes; it's even natural to be afraid of it. Living eucharistically is not always easy. We should take comfort in remembering that faith does not mean never doubting and never being afraid, but remaining loving and trusting as Jesus did. That kind of openness is the context for experiencing the transformation that is the essence of eucharistic living.

Can we believe that the power of transformation occurs as God shapes everything now for our future redemption, even as He shaped the horror of Jesus' death to fit the glory of the resurrection?

Catching glimpses of this transformation

If we are truly open to living eucharistically, we will catch glimpses of this transformative process and the power of God in our life from time to time. It won't be steady and continuous, but signs will be there. We might think of these glimpses as little "epiphanies," manifestations, or shinings of the power of God. We might refer to them as "illuminations."

In a life lived eucharistically, we don't have to be in church, or at prayer, or even consciously thinking about God, for illumination to occur. Illumination doesn't occur only at those times, although hopefully, those occasions are at least sometimes moments of illumination. The point is that illumination involves making the connection between the moment we are in right now and a feeling that what is occurring now is larger than just this moment. It can be found in grasping the connection between the way we offer ourselves at Mass and the way we should offer ourselves outside of Mass, every moment of every day. When that connection is made, it's the experience of, "This is it! Now I get it! Now it's all clear! I've found it, and I wish it would never end, because now I know how to live my life; my life has real meaning, and purpose, and direction. I'm in the presence of what I have been looking for, something beautiful and holy." These "a-ha!" moments give us a sense of clarity and meaning, purpose and direction about our life. At those times, we are basking in the illuminative light of living eucharistically.

When have you "seen the light"—been illuminated—in this way, such that the living of your life as both a self-offering to God and to others really came together? Was it your wedding day? Or when you first told someone "I love you"? When you came back to Church after being away for a long time? When you finally accepted that you had to forgive someone, or had to be forgiven? Was it when your child was born, or baptized, or received First Holy Communion?

Perhaps it was when you felt like God suddenly gave you the solution to something that had been bothering you for a long time, or when you were asked for your advice, and you could not believe the wisdom that came out of your mouth. Maybe it was the time you took a walk and noticed the beauty of things you had never noticed before.

All the times when we see something more than our own human power at work, when a light clicks on in an unimagined way to suddenly make things clear, are moments of transformation, the moments of uniting the divine and the human in illumination. They are the moments when the ordinary bread and wine of our life are touched and made into the presence of God through the power of the Holy Spirit.

We are transformed by being members of the body of Christ

Living eucharistically can only be done by living in the midst of the community that is the body of Christ. Liturgy is always an action of the body, the Church, and so the celebration of the Eucharist is something that always transforms us more and more into being members of the body. Sometimes we forget that, though, and we wish that faith could be simply a case of "Jesus and me."

Who needs the Church? If I want to talk to God, I can go to God directly. Who are these priests and bishops to tell me what to do? The Church is just a business like anything else!

Ever heard those things said before, or things like them? Ever said them or thought them yourself? We might feel that way in moments of frustration, when it seems like the institutional Church has very little to do with God's love. Anyone who is wondering why they have to get an annulment, or who disagrees with the Church's teaching on sexuality or any area of morality, might feel that way. Many people, even some "very good Catholics," feel that their relationship with God is their own private business.

We can never give in to such erroneous thoughts, however, if we are going to truly live eucharistically. Living eucharistically means that we are inescapably bound to the Church. In the sixteenth chapter of Matthew's Gospel, Jesus tells Peter, "You are Peter and on this rock I will build my community. And the gates of the underworld can never overpower it." Jesus then goes on to give Peter the power and authority of the keys of the kingdom of heaven: "Whatever you bind on earth will be bound in heaven; whatever you loose on earth will be loosed in heaven." Obviously, then, Jesus Himself is establishing religious authority; that there be authority and structure in the Church is the will of Jesus Christ Himself.

So, that leaves us with an interesting question in terms of trying to live eucharistically: do we need an authority to find God, or is the mystery and depth of God richer and deeper than any Church authority?

The answer, of course, is "yes" to both of those! Jesus Himself attacked the kind of authority that pretended to have a monopoly on God, the religious hypocrisy so prevalent in His time. Religious leaders and Church authorities must always be vigilant to ensure that they are not exercising their office simply for their own power or self-aggrandizement. And, of course, it's true that in the long history of the Church there have been those popes, bishops, priests, deacons—and even lay leaders—who have misused their office in just that way. That does not negate the fact, however, that we need some kind of authority.

We already know that it was the will of the Lord Himself that an authority structure built on Peter be a part of the life of the Church—and that's a tremendous gift. We need that kind of authority because we need a place where the buck stops, lest everyone become their own pope, their own church. That's one of the things that defines us as Catholics and one of the things that is constitutive of eucharistic living—we don't splinter off or fragment into sub-groups, but rather we have to work out our differences, our problems, our tensions, within the one community of faith. Unity is essential in living eucharistically, a unity that has at its heart our unity with our bishop, who is in communion with all the other bishops of the world and with the first among the bishops, the Bishop of Rome, the pope.

That kind of authority is a gift because it constantly reminds us that we are always capable of something better. One of the things about the teachings and writings of Pope Benedict XVI, to use but the most recent example of the writings of our many popes, is that they give us a higher ideal to strive for. The official teaching of the Church gives us the larger picture, so that we can do what is truly right and good. For example, recall Pope Paul VI's *Humanae Vitae,* his encyclical letter on the regulation of birth. Reading that letter again, it's fascinating to see how the pope was so prophetic over 40 years ago, warning us against the dangers of losing an essential part of our humanity when we allow science and technology to become more important than the values that make sexuality human.

We need a teaching authority to help us figure out what to do and how to live eucharistically. This involves a properly-formed conscience, one that is formed by the faith that accepts the presence of Christ in the Church and the power of the Holy Spirit that guides the teaching authority of the Church. This is how we remain in contact with the Living Tradition that is the very teaching of Jesus Christ, a tradition that teaches us how to live so that we might be truly happy and fulfilled, how to live in a way that is meaningful and filled with joy and hope, and how to live with our hearts and minds open to the presence and love of God that is right here in our midst. We cannot truly live eucharistically without this.

We have a reminder of this within the Eucharistic Prayer. When we mention the name of the pope and our bishop in the Eucharistic Prayer, we are doing something more important than making a spiritual remembrance. Actually, we are making an important statement about the unity and authenticity of our Catholic faith as it is connected with the official structure founded by Jesus Himself. In other words, every Eucharist is a reminder that we are all in this together. Living eucharistically is not only communion with the Risen Lord who feeds us with his Body and Blood, but it is also communion with Christ's Body, the Church, which includes all its visible authority structures. Can we trust and believe that, even with all its human limitations and flaws, the Church and all its structures, because it is founded by Jesus Who is always present in His Church, can be an avenue to probe the unfathomable mystery of God's endless and inconceivable love for each and every one of us? Can we accept that full transformation in the Spirit can only occur within the body that is the Church, a body that has visible and hierarchical structures of leadership and authority?

4

BREAKING

Connecting Everyday Life with
the Fraction Rite

❧

WE now come to the third of the four-fold actions, the action of breaking, called the Fraction Rite. This is the part of the Mass where the priest breaks the host into pieces, and during which the assembly sings or says the Lamb of God litany.

Unfortunately, this ritual action is sometimes minimized, much to the detriment of the full liturgical expression of the four-fold actions. The bishops of the United States, in their document *Introduction to the Order of Mass: A Pastoral Resource of the Bishops' Committee on the Liturgy,* a document that comments on the *General Instruction of the Roman Missal* and gives helpful direction to enacting the ritual celebration of the Eucharist as fully as possible, offers these helpful observations in paragraphs 130 and 131:

> This characteristic action of Christ [breaking of bread] at the feeding of the multitude, at the Last Supper, and at his meals with the disciples after his resurrection in the days of the Apostles gave its name to the entire celebration of the Eucharist. The natural, the practical, the symbolic, and the spiritual are all inextricably linked in this most powerful symbol. Just as many grains of wheat are ground, kneaded, and baked together to become one loaf, which is then broken and shared out among many to bring them into one table-fellowship, so those gathered

are made one body in the one bread of life that is Christ (see 1 Cor 10:17). In order for the meaning of this symbolism to be perceived, both the bread and the breaking must be truly authentic and recognizable. The Eucharistic bread is to "have the appearance of food" and is to be made so that it can be broken and distributed to at least some of the members of the congregation.[8]

We see, then, how important this action of breaking is, as in the early Church "the breaking of the bread" was one of the names given to the celebration of the Eucharist. Originally, it had a practical function, since, after being consecrated, the loaves of bread that had been brought by the people as offerings had to be divided up in order to be distributed to them as Holy Communion. Yet, beyond this practical function, as the above reminds us, there is a tremendous spirituality of the Eucharist being expressed.

First and foremost is the idea of unity, as highlighted by the above reference to Paul's first letter to the Corinthians. As there is one bread (one loaf), so too we, though many, are one single body. The breaking of the bread reminds us that we are all "fragments" who only find our true identity as members of the one bread that is the body of Christ, as we minister to one another. After all, how is it possible to help someone who always has it all together, who is never fragmented, and who never has the room to let anyone else in? How can God get in, if we are so complete in and of ourselves that there are no broken places for Him to enter? Living eucharistically means we take the greatest risk of all: we admit to each other that we are incomplete, and that we need each other, because all of us together make up the body of Christ.

---

[8] Pastoral Liturgy Series 1, United States Conference of Catholic Bishops (Washington D.C., 2003).

Brokenness and participation in the mystery

There is, unfortunately, a common practice that diminishes the ritual expression of our participation in the Eucharist, and that is the practice of regularly going to the tabernacle to use hosts already-consecrated for distribution during Holy Communion. This practice short-circuits the liturgical expression of the people's participation in the offering of the sacrifice. Recall the action of the Mass about which we have spoken so often: the central act of participation is the joining of everyone's sacrifice to the sacrifice of Christ, as that offering is lifted up to the Father "through Christ, with Him, and in Him, in the unity of the Holy Spirit." The bread and wine brought to the altar symbolize our offering and our participation in the offering of the sacrifice, the bringing of our lives to the altar. Those gifts of bread and wine are then prayed over in the action of blessing during the Eucharistic Prayer, as Christ's Paschal Mystery is recalled and made present; in that Eucharistic praying, the bread and wine are transformed into the Body and Blood of Christ. Those gifts of bread and wine, transformed into the Real Presence of Jesus, will now be given back to the assembly as food from heaven, food of which they are to partake, as the culmination of their participation in the sacrifice and as a sign of their oneness in Christ. The very point to be emphasized is the connection between *this* bread and wine that has been taken to the altar, prayed over in blessing, transformed, and broken, as the *same* bread and wine that will now be given. When the Communion that is given and received is not the same gift that has been offered at that sacrifice, the ritual expression of the assembly's full participation in the offering of the sacrifice is frustrated and short-circuited.

Receiving Holy Communion from consecrated hosts taken from the tabernacle is still Holy Communion, of course.

Consecrated hosts in the tabernacle are truly the Body (and Blood) of Christ, His Real Presence. However, the liturgical sign being expressed by the action is more akin to simply "receiving Communion," instead of the full expression of "receiving Communion from the same elements that have been offered as a sign and as the culmination of participating in the sacrifice offered here and now."

The *General Instruction of the Roman Missal* says it quite directly, in paragraph 85:

> It is most desirable that the faithful, just as the priest himself is bound to do, receive the Lord's Body from hosts consecrated at the same Mass and that, in the instances when it is permitted, they partake of the chalice ... **so that even by means of the signs Communion will stand out more clearly as a participation in the sacrifice actually being celebrated.**[9] (emphasis added)

The United States bishops state it even more clearly: "The faithful are not ordinarily to be given Holy Communion from the tabernacle with hosts consecrated at a previous Mass."[10]

Given the size of our liturgical assemblies, it may be impossible to actually break loaves of bread into enough pieces to accommodate the number of people; we do not want this part of the Mass to become disproportionate to the other parts, and it should not be unduly prolonged. What can be done, however, is that enough individual hosts for the communion of the assembly can be brought forward in one large vessel. Then, during the Fraction Rite, the hosts are apportioned out into the

---

[9] Liturgy Documentary Series 2, United States Conference of Catholic Bishops (Washington D.C., 2003).

[10] *Introduction to the Order of Mass: A Pastoral Resource of the Bishops' Committee on the Liturgy.* Pastoral Liturgy Series 1. (Washington, D.C.: United States Conference of Catholic Bishops, 2003).

smaller vessels that will be used for the distribution of Holy Communion. When the consecrated bread actually needs to be either broken or at least in some way divided, the Fraction Rite can then take on its rightful significance in terms of the unity of the liturgical assembly and in terms of the people's sharing in the offering of the sacrifice actually being celebrated.

Such fractioning, done carefully and deliberately by the priest and observed by the liturgical assembly, can also then take on other layers of spiritual significance that connect with our living eucharistically. Specifically, as the breaking action will inherently lead to the giving action, so we can rejoice that out of our brokenness we can give to each other.

Brokenness can mean transformation to abundant new life

I have already mentioned how I have followed the life and career of singer Olivia Newton-John, referring, as well, to her being diagnosed with breast cancer. There's a story she has told of what a close friend of hers, Jim Chuda, said to her at the time of her diagnosis. Jim and his wife Nancy had recently lost their five-year-old daughter Collette to a rare form of cancer. His statement to his good friend Olivia was, "Congratulations. Now you will grow."

At face value, that might sound like a strange, if not somewhat callous, remark to make. It is not, however, a strange way of looking at adversity for those who are living eucharistically and for those who define their lives as being in the pattern of the Paschal Mystery. Those who are living eucharistically understand that, when we are united to Christ, brokenness leads to growth because Christ's Good Friday led to Easter Sunday; Christ's cross led to resurrection. If we are united to Him, then His pattern is our pattern. We do not accomplish such transformation, of course; only God can bring it about. Living eucharistically is all about the trust and confidence that, indeed, God will transform brokenness into new life.

Such transformation occurred within my own family, as I'm sure it has in many of yours. Over the course of seven years, my mother suffered with a form of dementia that slowly robbed her more and more of being able to do things. Eventually, she was no longer able to speak at all and, at the end of her life, was bedridden. Now, in my family, my mother was always a strong presence in the household who handled and supervised most, if not all, of the daily tasks of family life. She had to; my father was often out working two jobs. She handled all the finances, and my father would often joke that he did not even know how to write a check! Yet, as my mother's disease progressed, something very beautiful happened. As she was able to handle less and less, it was amazing to see my father handle more and more. All of my siblings and I were adults and out of the house by this time, and it was as though our parents' fifty years of marriage came to fruition in a divine reversal: as my mother had taken care of all of us and managed the family all those years, now it was our dad's time to take care of her, as best as he was able for as long as he was able.

It was terribly hard for all of us to see our mother slowly disappearing before our eyes; she was not able to carry on a conversation for the last four or five years of her life, and eventually was not able to recognize anyone except my father. Yet, in the process of letting our mother go and coming to accept that she would never be the same, a transformation came about in our family. Each of us, by stepping up to the plate, in both practical and emotional ways to fill in the void left by the diminishing capacities of our wife and mother, saw new dynamics and new relationships emerge. There was a grace-filled transformation in our family as we drew closer in faith and in acceptance of what was taking place. That same transformation-in-the-midst-of-brokenness re-occurred for my brothers and me approximately six years later, as we accompanied my father on his journey of dealing with terminal lung cancer.

When we live eucharistically we are able to use the broken places as opportunities for growth and new life as this transformation is grounded in the very fabric of Christian living.

Brokenness does not change the truth of who we are

Recall that a basic theme of this book has been that living eucharistically is all about becoming the truth of who we are called to be, the body of Christ in the world—the presence of Jesus. Recall as well that one of the Scriptural foundations for this can be found in the first letter of Peter, chapter 2, verses 9-10:

> But you are "a chosen race, a royal priesthood, a holy nation, a people claimed by God as his own possession," so that you may proclaim the praise of him who called you out of darkness into his marvelous light. Once you were not a people, but now you are God's people.

That identity is an identity given to us in our baptism, an identity into which we are supposed to be transformed more and more fully through living a life of holiness and, most especially, through our participation in the Eucharist. Nothing can ever take that away. Our sinfulness might obscure that identity; we might reject it by turning away from God. The fact is, though, that from God's point of view, we will always be His beloved, since we have been created in His image and likeness, and through the waters of baptism have taken on the life of His Son. Living eucharistically means recognizing that the brokenness of the eucharistic bread is constitutive of its meaning as Eucharist. It is not only the whole loaf or the unbroken loaf that is recognizable as the Body of Christ; it is also the broken pieces—the fragments—that are His Real Presence. Despite the brokenness that we experience in our life—brokenness of sin, of sickness, of hatred, of anger, of betrayal, of everything that frustrates our happiness and the achieving of our full potential before God—the truth of who we are as being loved by God does not change.

This was brought home to me in an incident recalled by Christopher Reeve in his book *Still Me*. Reeve was the actor who became famous portraying Clark Kent/Superman in movies in the 1970s and 1980s. On Memorial Day in 1995 Reeve was participating in a horseback riding competition and was suddenly thrown head-first from his horse. The accident left him paralyzed. In *Still Me*, Reeve relates the events of the scene that took place with his wife Dana shortly after the accident:

The doctors had explained my condition, and now I understood how serious it was. This was not a C5-C6, which means you're in a wheelchair but you can use your arms and breathe on your own. C1-C2 is about as bad as it gets. Why not die and save everyone a lot of trouble? Dana came into the room. She stood beside me, and we made eye contact. I mouthed my first lucid words to her: "Maybe we should let me go." Dana started crying. She said, "I am only going to say this once: I will support whatever you want to do, because this is your life, and your decision. But I want you to know that I'll be with you for the long haul, no matter what." Then she added the words that saved my life: "You're still you. And I love you."[11]

---

[11] (New York: Random House, 1998), pp. 31-32.

As the bread is being broken at Mass, can we hear God saying: *No matter what brokenness is in your life, no matter what your sins are, no matter what obstacles you are facing—you're still you, and I love you.* With that assurance from God, we can trust that He will be able to transform our brokenness and make something new out of it, as surely as He took the brokenness of Jesus' crucifixion and transformed it into the glory of resurrected life. Living eucharistically means having the trust that God looks beneath our brokenness and our sinfulness and still loves the son or daughter He created, seeing our beauty and innocence, wanting us to be redeemed and made whole.

Brokenness can unite us to others

Living eucharistically demands that we be strong enough to face our brokenness and not deny the many different ways that it manifests itself. It's natural to want to keep our distance from anything that is associated with human brokenness or poverty. Don't we all like to be associated with the "winners," the "in crowd"? Our society places so much emphasis on being beautiful, being in style, and always fitting in, and, even though Christians are supposed to have a different set of values, we nonetheless often buy right into it.

Eucharistic living confronts us with all the ways we selfishly seek to insulate and separate ourselves from the afflictions and brokenness of life, either our own or someone else's.

A theme that runs throughout Mark's Gospel is that we can only fully understand Jesus after He goes to the cross. This is the reason behind what is referred to as "the Messianic secret," i.e., Jesus telling His disciples not to tell anyone about Him after He healed someone or after some other miracle (see Mark 7:31-37 as one example). With this motif of the Messianic secret, Mark is trying to show us that Jesus is the Messiah not just because He heals, but also because He allows Himself to be wounded. Jesus is the Messiah not because He is a wonder-worker, but because He goes to the cross, suffers, and dies. Rather than fleeing from human brokenness, Jesus embraces it, and, in being broken—in being crucified—He is raised up to new life.

This is the Good News: God came to transform and save the broken. The challenge to embrace every time we celebrate the Eucharist, indeed, the challenge of eucharistic living, is to realize that there is no separation between "us" and "them," namely, between those who are poor and broken and those who are not, because we are all poor; we are all broken. In different ways we all have wounds that need to be healed by God, be they physical, emotional, or spiritual. But, to be healed by God, we must first admit that we are broken. Eucharistic living occurs within the union of our common brokenness.

God's grace is at work in our brokenness

Since broken bread is of the essence of the grace, life, and presence of Jesus in the Eucharist, then we should realize that our brokenness is not incompatible with grace-filled moments of God doing extraordinary things in the midst of that brokenness. Yes, it can seem like a huge contradiction that human brokenness and divine grace exist side-by-side, but does it really seem that strange when the very heart of our faith is the most intense contradiction of all: that death leads to life? Eucharistic living occurs under the shadow of the greatest paradox of all! My coming to terms with what it means to deal with such paradoxes in life is probably why penguins are my favorite animal. I think it's precisely because I find them to be such a contradiction, such a paradox: they're absurd, funny, and yet at the same time dignified, almost regal.

How do we think of God's glory manifesting itself to us? Our first inclination might be to see God's glory when everything is going right, when we feel strong and in control of our life. In true eucharistic living, however, God's glory does not manifest itself only when things are going right; in fact, God's glory most powerfully manifests itself in ways that we don't even think of as glorious. Sometimes, God's glory shines through most powerfully when we feel most insecure, and, yes, even absurd!

In St. John's Gospel, 13:31-35, Jesus proclaims, "Now has the Son of Man been glorified, and in him God has been glorified." For St. John, however, this glorification means crucifixion, going to the cross. The glorified Jesus is the crucified-risen Jesus. The glory is found in His unselfish love, in giving His life away, in allowing His body to be broken. What's more, He tells His followers to do the same thing. "I give you a new commandment: love one another; you must love one another just as I have loved you" (Jn 13:34).

Can we look at the crucified Jesus and see glory? Do we accept that it is only out of death—the gift of His life—that new life can come? Or, do we think glory is only the new life? In other words, do we miss the meaning of the *passage*, the *passing through*, that has to be an integral part of eucharistic living?

The mystery is that God's glory is seen not in God's power to take away all our problems and difficulties and absurdities, but rather to *re-create us through them, to bring new life out of them*. Recall that in the Acts of the Apostles, Paul and Barnabas plainly told the people, "We must all experience many hardships before we enter the kingdom of God" (14:22). They did this not to emphasize the hardships, but as a way of encouragement. In that same chapter, when they return home after a journey of spreading the faith, they reported what God had done through them and what God had helped them to accomplish. The point for them was not the hardships themselves, but what God brought out of those hardships. In other words, like dignity and absurdity existing side-by-side, God brings about good in the midst of our hardships.

A large part of eucharistic living is the willingness and ability to put together two things we would not think of as ordinarily going together: absurdity and dignity, Good Friday and Easter Sunday; cross and resurrection, death leading to new life; ordinary bread and the Body of Christ, ordinary wine and the Blood of Christ, ordinary eating and drinking, and intimate union and communion with the life of God.

How many times in our life has the moment of greatest absurdity—when we have been the lowest—actually been the turning point leading us to the point of greatest dignity? Those familiar with the disease of alcoholism know that an alcoholic has to hit rockbottom before she or he will seek help. How many times does a debilitating disease—Alzheimer's or cancer—become an occasion of great love, the glory of tenderness and devotion as family members come together to care for their loved one?

God's glory is manifested in the reality that obstacles can lead to transformation in our life. God's glory is not in avoiding the cross, but in going to the cross, dying with Jesus, and then rising with Him. Every Eucharist is an occasion to put together two things that don't go together. We say that bread and wine become Jesus' Body and Blood; we say that by entering into His death by sharing in the Eucharistic meal, we rise with Him into glory!

Brokenness can lead us to the deeper reality of true healing

The breaking of the bread can also remind us to look beyond the brokenness to the life that exists on a deeper level. A person can be broken on one level (the physical level, for example) yet still be whole spiritually. Likewise, even though someone might not be cured, it doesn't automatically mean they have not been healed.

There's a difference between being *cured* and being *healed*. The Gospels are replete with stories of Jesus curing people of their illnesses. Mark's Gospel, for example, reminds us that to see Jesus simply as a wonder-worker is to run the danger of misunderstanding what He is all about. Mark is very clear and consistent in telling us that we should not believe in Jesus only because of physical cures; that's not what makes Him the Son of God. The healings are only signs, signs that should lead to faith. What makes Jesus the Son of God is His going to the cross—His dying and rising. That's why at the end of Mark's Gospel it is only the Roman Centurion at the foot of the cross who can rightly say, "In truth this man was the Son of God" (Mk 15:39). He sees Jesus not as the wonder-worker, but as the crucified one. The healing miracles are previews that foreshadow the ultimate miracle of true healing, the Paschal Mystery.

We need to see that Paschal Mystery at work in our own life situation if we are truly going to live eucharistically. It's not that there is anything wrong with asking God to cure us or our loved ones. Nor can we ever presume to know or limit how God does or does not work in the world. But we do have to be careful not to look for the miraculous razzle-dazzle or speedy solution. In a world of fast-food, instant technology and internet access, it might be easy to forget that there's more to faith than quick fixes; there is more to healing than physical cure. I can honestly say that I have been with many people who were never cured, but were definitely healed.

When a physical cure does not occur, does that mean we have not prayed hard enough? That we said the wrong prayers? That God was not listening? That it was God's will for us to suffer for some reason? That God gave us the sickness?

The answer to all of those questions is, of course, a resounding no. True healing is not in the quick-fix or in the flashy cure but in the *process, the journey* of going to the cross with Jesus and rising to new life with Him. That's what we celebrate in each and every Eucharist.

The brokenness that is ritually enacted at the celebration of the Eucharist can remind us that our humanity is more than just the sum total of our physical well-being. We can really be healed, not just cured, if we believe that the power of the Kingdom of God, a power stronger than death, is at work in us even in the midst of our pain. We are truly healed, and not just cured, when we can hand ourselves over in trust to the God Who will raise us up, but Who can do so only if we first go to the cross with His Son. The breaking of the bread at Mass can remind us that in this life a certain amount of brokenness is inescapable. Remember, the risen Jesus still bore the marks of His crucifixion in His risen body. Brokenness is a constitutive element of deeper life in eucharistic living.

Our brokenness leads us to knowing who Jesus is

Ultimately, then, the brokenness that is an element of living eucharistically forces us to come to terms with an answer to the central question posed by the Gospels concerning Jesus: "Who do you say that I am?" Living eucharistically means that our answer to that question is an answer based in the truth of Jesus as Savior, rather than in some false image of God. Our answer to that question must accept the way God works in the world, not becoming frustrated because He does not work as we think He should. Our answer must be a eucharistic answer, for eucharistic living.

For example, oftentimes we insist that God's answer to all our problems must be to make all the evils and brokenness and sinfulness go away; we insist that salvation has to be seen in terms of victory, triumph, and power: "God equals success." But, what if God's definition of victory, triumph, power, and success is not the same as ours? What if, instead of God taking us *out* of evil, and brokenness, and sinfulness, God's answer is to overcome it by *coming into it with us*? What if God's answer is simply that He will keep loving us and guiding us *through* our frustration, our pain, and our cross, rather than taking it away?

We certainly have the choice not to accept this and to try to reinvent God, and come up with a so-called better way. We can try to find our salvation in other things, in short-cuts that provide a quick and temporary relief from our problems and our brokenness, but that will never work in the long run. If we choose those options, we will miss out on the adventure of new life that God has created for us when we trust in His way—we will miss out on eucharistic transformation. Indeed, we are called to simply take up our cross and follow Jesus. To take up our cross is to dare to believe that new life comes only by confronting our frustration, and pain, and brokenness, and sinfulness, not by denying it or avoiding it. A good example of this can sometimes be found in the hard work a man and a woman must do in working through problems in their marriage. For new life to come about in the healing of a troubled marriage, both the husband and the wife must first admit the exact nature of their difficulties and each one must examine how he or she is at least partly at fault. Engaging in honest self-examination rather than blaming someone else is a concrete way of taking up one's cross. It is one way we can dare to see things from God's perspective, a perspective where transformation occurs, if we trust in Him.

On our part, it might mean we need to make a complete turnaround, a fundamental shift, a true conversion, in what we think it means to be saved. It means being comfortable living with a riddle that has no final explanation: the riddle that says you find your life by losing it, that death is a way to life, and that growth comes out of suffering. Think back on some of the worst times in your life; isn't it true that it was exactly those times that, in the long run, led to something new and better, and times, therefore, that were actually true moments of life-giving grace? Trusting in the grace that is at work in those times is living the riddle of the cross, and therefore, it is living eucharistically. Jesus was able to have that trust; are we?

5

GIVING

Connecting Everyday Life with
the Communion Procession and
Reception of Holy Communion

❧

WE come to the last of the four-fold actions, that of giving. The giving action is ritually enacted in the Communion Procession as all come forward to receive the Body and Blood of the Lord, sharing in the heavenly banquet as the culminating sign of participating in the sacrifice.

Never underestimate what it means to process to the altar to share in the food from heaven. The Communion Procession is not a mere functional going forward to get something; rather, it is the pilgrimage of the people of God on their way to the Kingdom. As we process forward singing (we should be joining in the singing during Communion as a sign of our unity with our brothers and sisters—the time for individual, silent reflection is during the period of silence after everyone has received Communion and after the singing has ended), we should make the connection with our eucharistic living: Christian life is not about sitting around and getting served, but it is about constantly moving toward the Lord with our brothers and sisters. Our faith must be put into action, and everything we say and do in our life should be a movement toward Christ.

In the giving action of the Mass—the reception of Holy Communion—we receive back what has been touched and given new meaning by God. True, in one sense, everything is the same: we have the same problems, we have the same search for meaning, the same failings as we had when we began Mass. But in another sense, things are not the same—they are transformed, made new. Isn't that true of the bread and wine—it's the same, but it's been made new? In traditional theological language, transubstantiation has taken place: the outer appearances of bread and wine remain, but the substances of both, the reality of what they are, have been transformed into the Real Presence of Jesus, His risen, glorified, transformed Body and Blood.

Dying and rising has taken place, if we have fully, consciously, and actively participated. If we have truly joined the sacrifice of our life, lived eucharistically, with Christ's sacrifice made present through the power of the Holy Spirit, then our life and our offering have been merged with God, and transformed and redeemed. The problem, the tragedy, the failing, is still there, but somehow, because we have given it to God and He has touched it, it has new meaning. We can go on for another day, for another week. Somehow, we can have just a little more hope. Somehow, we can believe that there is meaning and value to life. Why? It is because Jesus nourishes us with the gift of Himself, and shares His very life with us, and that nourishment is given to us not as individuals, but as members of His body. We eat and drink with others who share the bread and wine of our sorrows and the bread and wine of our joy, the bread and wine of our hopes and the bread and wine of our fears. Most importantly, Jesus Himself is the one to share that with us because He is there! Jesus' Real Presence is a presence that is not just "there," but one that is a dynamic, active, communicative Presence where He is always giving Himself to us. In the celebration of the Eucharist, we encounter Love Itself, a love that is so great, so big, so vast, that it can't be explained, and it can't even be understood—it can only be eaten and drunk. Living eucharistically means that we embody and enflesh that love when we leave the Mass, as we give ourselves away to others so that they are nourished by our love, our compassion, and our forgiveness.

Living eucharistically means freely sharing ourselves abundantly, not stingily

I collect comic books as a hobby. What is it that makes a comic book, or any collectible item, "valuable?" It's "valuable" because it's rare—because no one else, or very few other people have it. If it's commonplace and easily obtainable, it's worth less money. It's the "rare" and "limited" editions collectors seek out.

While that might be okay for collecting things as a hobby, it's a problem when we apply that principle to other parts of our life. If we do that, then our whole outlook, not only toward collectibles, but toward everything, becomes one of competition or jealousy, where the important thing is not just to have something or to be something, but to have more of it, or to be better at it than everyone else. This makes me think of an old saying I once heard about the business world: "Competition brings out the best in products, but the worst in people."

Eucharistic living is a whole other way of approaching life; it's the exact opposite of the competition, jealousy, and arrogance of "it's mine, not yours" that we often live out in so many ways in our life. Living eucharistically gives us the perspective that everything in life—be it a material item, or a talent, or a relationship—is ultimately a gift from God to be freely shared with others, not as one's own exclusive possession.

Accepting goodness as a gift and sharing it, rather than jealously controlling it, is exemplified in an episode in the eleventh chapter of the Book of Numbers. In that Scripture passage, Eldad and Medad receive the gift of God's spirit and begin to prophesize, but others are jealous because Eldad and Medad were not part of the "in" group. Some people felt that Eldad and Medad should not be allowed to speak in God's name. The same thing is at work in chapter 9 of Mark's Gospel, when the disciples try to stop someone who is not part of their group from acting in Jesus' name.

The responses of both Moses and Jesus are the same in those two Scripture passages: don't stop them; don't be jealous, intolerant, or arrogant; don't think that you have a monopoly on God; what's important is that God's work is being done, not who is doing it; wherever there is goodness and love, it is of God.

True eucharistic living will confront us with all the ways we are jealous, arrogant, and intolerant because we don't accept the gifts of others, and instead feel we have to control them or compete with them. Certainly, we do it with knowledge and with information: "I know something you don't, and I'll keep you in the dark because it gives me a sense of power to do so." We do it with relationships: "I know so-and-so; we're buddies and you're not, so that makes me important." We do it in families, with unhealthy ways of relating: children might compete for their parents' affection, or parents might withhold love and acceptance as a way of manipulating their children. We do it with religion, too: "I'm a good Catholic. I say my prayers and I go to Mass every week. I'm supposed to receive blessings, but not you, because you're not as religious as I am." We can even do it with ministry: "I'm a lector; I'm an extraordinary minister of Holy Communion; I'm a volunteer; I'm a deacon; I'm a priest; I'm on the 'inside track.' "

Whenever we foster exclusivity instead of inclusivity, whenever we foster an unhealthy clique and exclusive ownership, we miss out on what is liberating and life-giving, a eucharistic spirituality that says, "Hey, the whole thing is a gift from God anyway! It's not mine, it's not yours; we are merely stewards."

That's the challenge of every celebration of the Eucharist and the challenge of eucharistic living. That, in fact, is the eucharistic spirituality we should live every day: living in a way that embodies the truth that what makes something valuable is not when it is scarce, but when everyone shares in it; recognizing that everything we have has been given to us not as our own private possession to make us feel secure or superior, but as a gift from God to be freely shared. When we can truly live that way, we will be living eucharistically.

Living eucharistically shows how the Eucharist is true food

At certain times, there's nothing like junk food. We often reach for it when we need a quick fix, a burst of energy. But that's exactly the problem with junk food, isn't it? It gives us a sugar high, but it doesn't really nourish us. In fact, sometimes we actually feel worse after coming down from the sugar high. We're better off reaching for real food; it's more sustaining.

The Eucharist is food that sustains us in living eucharistically. Jesus as the Bread of Life is the true bread—the only true food—that nourishes us on our journey. That's because Jesus' bread is the bread of relationship with God, a relationship rooted in the offering of ourselves as sacrifices acceptable to God. That's why the "giving" action of the Eucharist is the culmination of our participation in the offering of the sacrifice: because the true food we receive strengthens us to live a true life, a life of self-giving.

To believe and share in Jesus as the bread come down from heaven (see John 6, the Bread of Life discourse) is to believe something not only about Jesus, but also something about our own life. It means knowing what we are really hungry for. It means recognizing that we are on a journey, and that we should be going somewhere in life. It means searching for the real food that gives true nourishment, as opposed to the junk food that provides a quick fix, but does not really sustain us.

We can find a summary of eucharistic living in Saint Paul's letter to the Ephesians, chapter 4, verse 32: "Be generous to one another, sympathetic, forgiving each other as readily as God forgave you." When we feed our hearts and minds with other things—the junk food of egotism, domination, possessiveness, illusion, jealousy, hatred, competition, bitterness, anger, harsh words, slander, malice—they might produce a momentary high and meet a distorted emotional need, but they will ultimately fail to nourish us on the journey toward true life. Authentic nourishment comes from living the life of Jesus Christ. Authentic eucharistic living comes from surrendering ourselves to the Father through Christ, with Him and in Him.

Receiving Holy Communion is food for the journey of eucharistic living

I can remember as a child that whenever we would get ready to take a car trip to upstate New York (I grew up on Long Island, and one of my uncles lived on a farm in the Catskill Mountains), a very important part of the trip would be the preparation—getting together the snacks for the 3½-hour ride: pretzels, soda, Fudge Town cookies, Twizzlers, Twinkies, and sugar-coated jelly spearmint leaves. (And, of course, there was always the plastic garbage bag to take along, in case anyone got sick . . . I wonder why?) All of that would be gathered as the all-important food for the journey.

Christ Himself, as our Eucharistic Bread, as the bread come down from heaven, is the food for our journey: our journey toward eternal life, but also our journey of living eucharistically here and now.

This journey here and now to Jesus and with Jesus is not one we make alone. Let's recall now the passage from 1 Corinthians 10:17 referred to earlier: "And as there is one loaf, so we, although there are many of us, are one single body, for we all share in the one loaf." St. Paul was writing to the Church community in Corinth because they held an individualistic attitude toward the Eucharist, i.e., participating in Eucharist and receiving the Body and Blood of Christ were just a matter of their own personal salvation: "Jesus and me." That's a misguided emphasis that still plagues us today. Paul is very strong in teaching that the Eucharist unites us not only to Christ, but also to our brothers and sisters in the Christian community—and with that unity comes the obligation of love.

The journey of living eucharistically is the journey of doing what Jesus did: namely, giving our life to God by giving our life selflessly to our brothers and sisters. That's what we remember in every Eucharist: that Jesus gave His life away in love (offering). At Mass, we unite ourselves to that offering, and we complete the action of joining our sacrifice to Christ's sacrifice by sharing in sacramental communion, the "giving" action of the four-fold actions.

However, we should also point out that the act of receiving communion also includes making an *active promise*. When we respond "Amen," our "Amen" affirms our belief not only in what it is (the Real Presence of the Body and Blood of the Lord), but also in what it means to be one with Christ in terms of the way one lives. The journey of eucharistic living involves the "Amen promise"—emptying ourselves of ourselves every day so that we can give ourselves away to others. It's a promise we make together as many parts of the one loaf, one body.

God makes a promise as He gives Himself to us in the Eucharistic food

One of the reasons that our "Amen" as a response to receiving Holy Communion should include the promise to live eucharistically is because God's gift of Himself in the Eucharist is His pledge and promise to us. Indeed, God has made a promise to each and every one of us to be always with us, to always give us new life, strength, hope, and peace. God has fulfilled this promise in Jesus Christ, and yet we also still await the fulfillment of those promises at the end of time with Jesus' second coming.

That means we live in both the present and in the new age that is to come. Living eucharistically means making the connection that the celebration of the Eucharist is a foretaste of the heavenly fulfillment yet to come in the Kingdom of God, and therefore involves living life with an openness and expectation of that heavenly fulfillment. It's as though eucharistic living always has a little bit of the season of Advent in it! It's as though we are standing in the dark, yet our faces are lit up because we are facing the sunrise. Consequently, all Christians must live as though the new dawn, the new age, was just around the corner. Eucharistic living means that no matter how involved we become in the affairs of this world, we never lose sight of the horizon of divine promises.

We must remember that ultimately salvation does not come from anything we do, but from what God does, the divine promises He always fulfills. We must accept that human achievement goes only so far, and, after that, we need God to intervene if true and lasting peace and happiness are to occur. Eucharistic living allows us to detect those hints or signals in our life by which God is calling us to rely on Him alone, instead of on something that is an illusion. Living eucharistically is to live believing in the fulfillment of God's promises that is yet to come.

Holy Communion is communion not only with the Lord, but also with each other

We have previously mentioned how our reception of Holy Communion is an act of union not only with the Lord, but also with our brothers and sisters in the body of Christ who also make up the parts of the one bread. Therefore, it is appropriate to reflect on both the spiritual meaning and the spiritual consequences of that radical oneness in the Eucharist—our oneness with each other not only in liturgical celebration, but also in the way we live life.

In many ways, this radical unity boils down to nothing more than having the right to expect the best from each other. A spiritually mature person recognizes that being part of a community to which we are responsible is a good thing. Accepting that our behaviors have consequences, and that we are answerable to a group, can help us to grow in spiritual and psychological maturity. Being willing to listen to the input of others, even their correction, is a powerful way to embrace the cross and a spirit of sacrifice, and to live eucharistically. Being accountable to and even corrected by a larger community—the eucharistic community—can help make us more authentically human.

Some mistakenly think that freedom means "doing whatever I want, whenever I want, and answering to no one." That's not freedom; that's license. True freedom is the ability to freely commit to a community where we are accountable to others and where we recognize the consequences of what we say and do. To live eucharistically is to acknowledge that we *need* a community of faith—we need others to show us what love is all about; community is not an option.

Perhaps the most striking example of this comes from the various 12-step groups such as Alcoholics Anonymous, Relationships Anonymous, and so on, in which people are challenged by others in brutal honesty to listen to each other and to get past their denial. These groups show us how we can be changed for the better when we allow ourselves to be confronted by the truth. If such change through truthful acceptance of one's faults and through accountability to others can happen in those groups, why can't the same happen in a community that is supposed to be the body of Christ?

We need each other to make sure we're loving God the right way; that's what Church is all about. Yes, it's difficult at times—as one sarcastic saying goes, "Church would be a great place if it weren't for all the other people." We would rather love God "alone" and not have to deal with our spouse, friend, parent, and the neighbor who always has a problem. Moreover, once we start to love in a truly Christian way, we will probably find the parameters to be limitless. Wouldn't it be easier to have a neat little formula: "all you have to do is this much and you have fulfilled your obligation." It would be so much easier to have clear limits, and not to go beyond what we are comfortable doing. We want to donate money, but only when we have extra, not when it will really cost us something. We feel good about bringing canned goods to a food pantry, but would we ever sit down for a meal with a homeless person? We may even consider going to Mass a burden if it interferes with something more "important"!

But is that what living in God's love is all about—a minimalism of obligation? Is that what living in eucharistic abundance is all about? God loves us without limits, God loves us unconditionally; God loves us even to the ultimate discomfort of letting His Son endure the cross so that we might have salvation. If God loves us that way, we also must love one another that way.

Unfortunately, I cannot give you a blueprint for how that applies in your life. There's no "one size fits all" pattern to follow. We have to figure it out as we go along. That's part of the journey of the Communion Procession of life, so to speak. It starts with recognizing the common obligation and the common vision to love by figuring it out together, as a Church, the Body of Christ.

That's why, for example, at the beginning of the Acts of the Apostles (1:15-26) it was so important to replace Judas with another apostle. Twelve was the number chosen by Jesus as a sign of the new Israel, the community of the new covenant. Twelve would be the sign of Jesus' community, born of the resurrection, to carry on His work and be His presence in the world. Matthias was chosen so that there would again be 12 apostles, a sign of fullness, and a sign of being authoritative witnesses to both the earthly ministry of Jesus and His resurrection. The Twelve would continue the mission of going out to the whole world *as one*! Jesus prays that His followers "may be one" just as He and the Father are one.

The Body of Christ here on earth continues the mission of Jesus as together we embody His love reaching out to others. Church is not "us and them," as though it were the ordained versus the laity, nor is it any one sub-group setting a course according to its own agenda. Rather, Church is the one Body of Christ, all of us together in communion with our bishop.

That's what we express in every Eucharist. Celebrating the Eucharist is not just an expression of one's own unity with the risen Jesus, but it's also a sign of unity with everyone else who shares in the sacred meal of His Body and Blood. Celebrating Mass and receiving Holy Communion is a communal action, an act of the body that we do together. Being a part of the community of the Church is no accident, and it's not just a nice thing to do; it's a necessary part of our salvation.

Doing Christ's work

The giving action of the Mass has important ramifications in our everyday life. Jesus shares His risen life with us as food in Holy Communion. We need to spend some time reflecting on what it means for us to have Him so freely and so completely share Himself and give Himself to us.

One thing it means is nothing less than this: through Christ's gift of the Eucharist, we have the potential to do in our life what He did in His. Jesus was fully God, but He was also *fully human*. We've got to stop keeping Jesus "up there" and to start understanding what it means that He comes "down here" to give Himself to us in Holy Communion.

Jesus was fully human—like us in everything and every way except sin. God became human so that human beings might become like Him. That's what sacraments are all about: "Christifying" us, making us into other Christs. That's what happens in every sacrament, and especially in the Eucharist: we are conformed more and more to the image and likeness of Jesus. Extraordinary! Amazing!! Incredible!!! We have to know that, internalize that, and be changed by it. More importantly, we must accept the responsibility for living that way.

Our task is to bring Christ to others, just as freely as He gives Himself to us. We must enlighten the darkness of this world with the light of Christ. We can do that only when Christ has transformed us, and we ourselves become that same light. Granted, we won't be performing any miracles; we are not divine, and we should not pretend to be. At the same time, though, we have to recognize our potential to participate in a real way in doing Christ's work in building up the Kingdom of God here and now in the places we go and the people with whom we interact every day. Eucharistic living demands that!

Connecting Baptism and Eucharist

It is fitting to recall, then, that every time we receive the Eucharist, we in essence renew our own baptism into Christ, the beginning of our sharing in the life of God and the beginning of our eucharistic life. Baptism leads to Eucharist. Essential to this baptismal/eucharistic identity is the notion of servanthood. We are called to be servants to God and to one another, as Jesus was; we are called to imitate His servanthood.

Christian servanthood is so much more than just "doing things for others," although that is certainly a part of it. Rather, that *doing* must flow from *being*: it must flow from a whole outlook and attitude that sees the larger background of God's plan for us, a plan where we become people who bring light and goodness into the world. It's an outlook that considers God's demands before our own. It's a life that is lived by asking what we can contribute to others, rather than what we can take from them. Indeed, like Jesus, we must do whatever is necessary, no matter how inconvenient—including going to the cross—in order to fulfill God's will. That's the life that has eucharistic spirituality at its core.

We don't receive Christ; Christ receives us

That's why, when all is said and done, it might be more appropriate to say that in Holy Communion, Christ receives us, rather than to say, we receive Christ. After all, it is His initiative in giving Himself to us that is the heart of the "giving" action. The goal is not for Christ to become part of us. The whole point is not His transformation, but our transformation! The goal of our reception of Holy Communion is the same as the goal for our entire eucharistic life: that we will be transformed into Him; that we will be grafted onto Him; that we will live His life; that we will become more and more like Him.

Ponder the spirituality: we don't receive Christ in Holy Communion; in Holy Communion, Christ receives us. What does that mean for you? How does that affect the way you live eucharistically?

6

GOING OUT AND
LIVING EUCHARISTICALLY

cr∿ɔ

LIVING eucharistically is all about the transformation that occurs when our lives enflesh the four eucharistic actions of taking, blessing, breaking, and giving. It is living that way that makes us who we are, and living that way is the truth of who we are called to be. The love of God given to us as food and drink in Jesus Christ's Body and Blood feeds us, and then we go out and feed each other. There's no room for spectators, however, neither at the liturgical celebration of the Eucharist, nor at the living of the eucharistic life. At both liturgy and in everyday life everyone must share in the activity of remembering Christ's Paschal Mystery, joining oneself to that offering by offering oneself, eating and sharing in the sacramental meal, and then going out and doing what they have celebrated. *The Body of Christ . . . I am/we are!*

Living eucharistically is a way of experiencing the resurrection in our midst

When we truly live a eucharistic life in all its fullness, we are living in the power of Jesus' resurrection from the dead. In fact, the eucharistic life is itself a sign of the power of the resurrection in our midst, a sign of Christ alive in us. It is His risen body that comes to us in the Eucharist. In order to appreciate living in His resurrection, however, it's appropriate to think about ways in which we have been raised up from death.

So, when have you been dead? When have you been entombed in fear and darkness? When have you been lost in despair and hopelessness? When have you been enslaved by something that was ruining your life? When have you been paralyzed by doubt and indecision? When have you felt totally powerless and helpless? When have you met death face-to-face because a loved one has died, or because a loved one's death, or perhaps even your own death, is imminent?

These are all different ways of being dead, ways of experiencing a diminishment of life, and ways of being caught in the dark fallout of death's effects. As we remember all these ways that the many forms of death intrude on our life, we must also remember that Jesus is the one who gives life in the face of death; He is the very life-giving presence of God. He brings life to those who are experiencing any kind of diminishment of life. In St. John's Gospel, the physical raising of Lazarus from death (Jn 11:1-44) is a sign that Jesus gives life to those who believe in Him.

Indeed, for a Christian, life itself means union with Jesus; life is incomprehensible and inconceivable without Him. Union with Him means to face death, in all its forms and manifestations, with Him. Eucharistic living is a life of dying and rising with Christ. To live eucharistically means really trusting that in those moments when we face some form of death, Jesus can do something for us that no one else and nothing else can, if we turn to Him.

Can we believe that Jesus gives us life *now*—not just when we die, but now, as we face death in its many forms of betrayal, hurt, sin, sickness, sadness, and brokenness? The truth is that Jesus does not take the dark moments away, and faith does not mean believing or hoping that He will. Instead, faith is believing that those moments, those deaths, are occasions for Him to raise us up with Him to new life. If we can let God have power over every part of our life, and if we can hand everything over to God with complete and utter trust, then we, like Lazarus, can be raised up and set free. Then, and only then, can we experience the intense inner power that we know to be the Holy Spirit, raising us up to new life even at the same time we are dying.

We feel the effects of this being raised up, this resurrection into the eucharistic life, when we finally find the strength to say "yes" to God in a new way. We are raised up and begin to live the eucharistic life when we can finally let go of that pattern of sin we have nurtured for so long. We are raised up and begin to live the eucharistic life when God helps us to finally forgive someone who brought us suffering. We are raised up and begin to live the eucharistic life when we find the strength to carry on with life in the face of tragedy. We are raised up and begin to live the eucharistic life when we continue to believe that God has not abandoned us, even when everything else points to giving up. We are living a risen, eucharistic life when we continue to affirm the goodness of life even in the face of death.

We cannot do those things or make those responses on our own; we can only do so because Jesus gives us the power to do so. Jesus' resurrected life inside us is that simple, perhaps unexplainable, presence which robs chaos of its power over us and trusts that God is still somehow at work, even in the midst of a life-diminishing situation. To live the eucharistic life is to live a life empowered by the risen Jesus.

Resurrection and living eucharistically

The eucharistic life that has faith in the resurrection of Jesus Christ at its core is much more than simply believing in an amazing fact, and it is more than experiencing the power of Jesus' resurrection by oneself alone. Instead, belief in Jesus' resurrection means accepting and being part of the eucharistic community born of the resurrection, relationships that can enliven every part of our life, now and forever. The eucharistic community that flows from the resurrection of Jesus and the way that community lives are the most powerful proofs that Jesus is indeed risen and that He gives life to His people.

The Acts of the Apostles, for example, shows us the continuing work of the risen Christ in His Church. Acts 2:42-47 gives us a summary of the characteristics of the early Church:

> They devoted themselves to the teaching of the apostles and to the communal fellowship, to the breaking of bread and to prayers. A sense of awe was felt by all for many wonders and signs were performed by the apostles. All the believers were together and owned everything in common. They would sell their property and possessions and distribute the proceeds to all according to what each one needed. Every day, united in spirit, they would assemble together in the temple. They would break bread in their homes and share their food with joyful and generous hearts as they praised God, and they were regarded with favor by all the people. And day by day the Lord added to those who were being saved.

Notice how in that description of the early Church the faithful actually lived a certain way because of their belief in the resurrection and their sharing in the Eucharist. Notice, too, there are four qualities of the Church in those times that are essential for true eucharistic living; those same four qualities should be reflected in our life. They are: openness to listening to the teachings of Jesus Christ; living a common life of caring for each other, expressed in concrete acts of sharing; being centered on the common meal of the breaking of the bread, the Eucharist; and being devoted to a life of prayer, thereby dedicating each day to God.

Living that way is what it's all about. The risen Jesus creates and empowers a new community to reflect His presence in the world. We must allow our gathering at the Eucharist each and every Sunday to remind us that we are that new community. We gather on the first day of the week, Sunday, as the disciples did; Jesus comes to be with us in word and in sacrament at Mass; and Jesus tells us to go out and live His way.

Eucharistic living involves the transformation of seeing the same things differently

When I was in the seminary studying for the priesthood, I had the opportunity to do the spiritual exercises of St. Ignatius of Loyola on a thirty-day silent retreat. Yes, that's right, it was 30 days of silence: no talking, except for one meeting per day with my spiritual director and my participation in daily Mass; no TV, no radio, no books except for the Bible and my spiritual journal; and, of course, in 1985, the internet, cell phones and iPhones were yet to be. It was one of the most remarkable experiences of my life, an experience that is still with me to this very day in many ways.

In addition to the spiritual benefits, I will always recall my drive out to the retreat house which was located on the south shore of Long Island; all I kept thinking was, I can't believe I'm doing this! What scared me most about the thought of the retreat, believe it or not, was that *it might really work!* I was afraid that those thirty days alone with God might really change me forever. All sorts of crazy ideas entered my mind; I was afraid something weird might happen. *What if I get swallowed up by God? What if I lose my personality? What if I am transformed into some glassy-eyed religious nut, walking around with a blank expression on my face?*

Needless to say, nothing like that happened, but I definitely was transformed, or, you might even say, transfigured. As we have seen, being transformed is essential to the eucharistic life. To be transformed or transfigured does not mean to become something different or to see something different. The presence of God and God's overwhelming love does not cause us to see different things; it causes us to see the same things differently. Let me give you an example of this from that same 30-day retreat.

I was eating breakfast one morning and looking out the window, when I noticed a squirrel gathering nuts and scurrying about. Suddenly, something clicked inside me. I realized that the squirrel was eating, and I was eating; the squirrel was dependent on food, and so was I. We were connected because we were both dependent. And, just as we both needed food to live, so too did we both depend on God for our existence.

At that moment, I became intensely aware of how much I needed God in my life. (Can you picture me telling this story to the average guy on the street? Me: *"Hey, Mister, did you know that that squirrel and I are connected?"* Man-on-the-Street: *"Yeah! You're both nutty!"*) The point is that I did not see anything out of the ordinary; I was just now seeing it differently. That insight, in fact, increased my love for God and influenced my prayer for the next several days as the thought, the joy, and the peace of that deepened awareness stayed with me; I had been transfigured.

Transfiguration means to see God at work in all things. It means to feel confirmed and energized in knowing that no matter what, God is always present and at work in us. Transfiguration means that the presence of God colors the way we see everything. It's essential to living eucharistically.

I have been using the words "transformed" and "transfigured" somewhat interchangeably in this reflection because I think there is a connection between the transformation that is a part of eucharistic living and transfiguration as we know it from the story of the Transfiguration from Luke's Gospel (chapter 9). At that point in Luke's Gospel, Jesus has just concluded His ministry throughout Galilee, and He has just told His disciples for the first time about the likelihood of His death. He goes up a mountain to pray, maybe praying over the choice He has to make: will He go on to Jerusalem, knowing that it will lead to a clash with the religious authorities and to His eventual death on the cross? Or will He go on in some other way? Of course, He chooses to go on to Jerusalem; this is the next section in Luke's Gospel. In this decision—continuing to say yes to His mission even though it will lead to His death—the future glory of the resurrection is glimpsed by Peter, James, and John as Jesus is transfigured.

Jesus' transfiguration tells us something about the way we are to live the eucharistic life. The believer sees the same sufferings and hardships, the same crucifixions that anyone else would see, but the believer *sees them differently*. In Jesus' journey, far from being a defeat, His crucifixion leads to glory; it brings about the Kingdom foretold through Moses and Elijah. Not even suffering and death can separate Jesus from God's love, nor can suffering and death defeat God's plan. Where others see senseless suffering, humiliation and defeat, the Christian sees the unfolding of God's Kingdom: "This is my Son, the Chosen One. Listen to him," says the voice from the cloud at the Transfiguration of Jesus (Lk 9:35).

Living eucharistically transforms us to see ordinary things differently, to see what we have always seen, but now in a new light. We are called to see new possibilities—God's possibilities—in what the rest of the world sees as ordinary.

When we suffer and encounter hardship, we are called to see not only the suffering and the cross, but to see how God is present, giving us new strength and new life. When we see someone in need, we are called to see Christ in that person and to serve that person. When we see divisions in our family, we are called to search out new possibilities for reconciliation. When we see failure, we are called to change that into an opportunity for growth and change. When we sin, we are called to see how much God loves the sinner and so repent. When we see hate and resentment, we are called to see how we can bring forgiveness, compassion and dialogue to the situation. Suffering, hardship, neediness, division, failure, sin, hate: these are the things of life that we are called to see differently, seeing them as opportunities to work with God in bringing about something new through love, trust, forgiveness, and compassion. Like Jesus, we are called to see our crosses changed into glorious resurrections, believing and trusting that God can do it when we cooperate with Him.

At Eucharist, ordinary bread and wine are transformed into the Body and Blood of Christ for us who believe. To an unbeliever, it is still ordinary bread and wine; for us, it's the very presence of God. That's the eucharistic life: to see God's presence in the ordinary, namely, in every person, every place, every thing, every sound, every sight, every word, every joy, every sadness, every suffering, every sin, every love, every person. We don't have to see different things to be holy; we just need to see the same things differently.

Living eucharistically means you have to be at Mass each and every Sunday

"You had to be there." You know what that saying means: it means you really cannot appreciate the situation, you cannot understand the joke, you cannot fully realize the irony, unless you were present at the right moment, and, in not being there, you missed out on something that cannot be fully explained or recaptured. Nothing can take the place of being there at the right time, in the right place, in the right situation.

I often think of that in terms of the post-resurrection story of Jesus and Thomas, and how that story connects both to the celebration of the Eucharist and to living the eucharistic life. Let's call to mind what Saint John tells us in chapter 20 of his Gospel. We encounter Thomas, who so often is maligned as "Doubting Thomas." He refuses to believe until he sees. The Scripture tells us that he was not there when Jesus came; Thomas was not with them on the evening of that first day of the week when the community was gathered together. But, you have to be there! So, how could he see Jesus? Then, one week later, the disciples were again gathered together, and this time Thomas was with them. Now he sees Jesus; now he encounters the mystery of the One who was crucified but is now risen; now he is able to say, "My Lord and my God!" You have to be there!

The point is that we encounter the presence of the Risen Jesus in the midst of the gathered community—you have to be there! The weekly gathering for Mass is an integral part of eucharistic living. Do we look on it that way, or do we take it for granted?

Sunday is the first holy day; it is the Lord's day. It is the day that is given a special place in the life of the Church because it is the day the Church gathers to celebrate the resurrection, the day we encounter the presence of the crucified-risen Jesus in our midst most powerfully, the day we see the Risen Jesus present among us most clearly. It is in this gathering that we sacramentally encounter His dying and rising; it is in this gathering that we die and rise with Him; it is in this gathering that we are nourished and find strength to live the Christian life; it is to this gathering that we bring the journey of our life and offer ourselves in union with Christ to the Father, so that our entire life, every moment of every day, might be transformed into an offering of our life to Christ.

Yet, the sad reality in our present society is that for many people coming each week to Mass is not a priority, given the hectic pace at which we live, the many demands placed upon families where both parents work and children are involved in a myriad of activities. Even families that do come to Mass regularly often do not come weekly—many people mistakenly feel that once or twice a month is enough.

But it's not! You have to be there, every Sunday, because it's there that we find our very identity. At Mass, we don't just do something; we become something. We become more who we are: people who live life every day as lives of offering, lives of self-giving and self-emptying, as Christ emptied Himself. At Mass we are supposed to be transformed into that living presence of Jesus, just as the bread and wine are transformed into His body and blood. Then and only then, because of our holy life, our transformed attitude, our ability to see and recognize Him, then and only then can we cry out with Thomas, "My Lord and my God." Then and only then can we live together "of one heart and mind," alleviating the poverty of the needy people among us because of the way we care for one another, as described in the previously-mentioned passage from the Acts of the Apostles. That passage gives us a description of Church that has been transformed into the living likeness of Jesus Christ because its members live His love.

Forming us and shaping us into what we are supposed to be, namely, the body of Christ in the world, is what's at the heart of being a part of Eucharist each and every Sunday, and is also at the heart of living eucharistically.

If we do that, we might just be surprised as to what happens to us, what changes inside us, week after week, almost imperceptibly, slowly, over time, as we continually hand ourselves over. Sunday should be seen as a day of spiritual formation in the eucharistic life. As a day of formation, Sunday should also be a day of transformation, where the selfishness of the "I" and the "me" become more and more the self-giving of the "we" and the "us." The "I" of egotistically looking out for "number one" should become transformed into the "we" of the Kingdom of God, where we selflessly live in union with God and with each other, giving our life to each other in imitation of Christ's sacrifice. That's how the transformative power of Sunday Eucharist, week after week, makes us who we are, the body of Christ in the world; that's how we live out our baptism as a kingdom of priestly people.

Even if we are weekly Mass-goers, it is good for us to be reminded why it is so important to do this. Anything we do often enough can become rote; we can forget the heart of what it's about; we might become centered only on the obligation, and not on the true meaning and spirit of what we do and why we do it. Those who attend Mass every week should continually recommit themselves to be totally present at worship—to fully, actively, and consciously participate with voices and bodies, with attitudes and with attentiveness, with preparation beforehand and with the living out of the Christian life afterward. It's a gift we give to one another to avoid passively attending Mass, wrapped up in our own little world. Eucharist is about praying together as one, as members of a body.

Next, it's everyone's job—not only Father's—to bring the message about Sunday Mass to neighbors, friends, and relatives. Let others know what difference going to Mass makes in your life—show them how your life is better as a result of celebrating the Eucharist. For indeed, what we do at Mass each Sunday is nothing less than the most important thing we do in our life, the thing that not only defines us as followers of Jesus, but also molds us in the way we live life as those followers. The celebration of the Eucharist is the place and activity by which we see clearly the crucified-risen one in our midst: Jesus, about whom each and every one of us cries out, "My Lord and my God!" But, in order to do that, you have to be there.

Living eucharistically means living in the community born of the resurrection

Those who live eucharistically find great strength, joy, and comfort living as members of the community born of Jesus' resurrection. Unfortunately, the necessity of being part of a community is a tough thing to buy into in today's world. We're used to being in the middle of midtown Manhattan, surrounded by throngs of people, yet not making any eye contact with any of them. We live in an individualized, technological society of e-mail, twitter, streaming videos, self-checkouts, and ATMs. We spend more time interacting with technology than with real people, and yet we wonder why we are lonely and feel disconnected!

Nevertheless, in the midst of this loneliness we are given a very special gift, the gift of the Church, the People of God: Church, the community of faith; Church, the people who come together all facing the same struggles and the same loneliness; Church, the people who live eucharistically as the body of Christ.

To overcome the loneliness of today's world we should seek the security and love of being connected to the Church. Faith cannot be privatized; we need to give each other the witness that Jesus is found in our gathering, and that only His presence can overcome the loneliness we feel. It is only through the Church—not as individuals, but as a people—that we most powerfully experience the Holy Spirit's gifts of excitement, exuberance, and enthusiasm.

The next time we are feeling an inescapable loneliness, we can turn to the most profound family we belong to, the family of the eucharistic Church. The body of Christ that celebrates the Eucharist is the abiding sign that we will never be abandoned by Jesus. Living our life in the midst of that eucharistic family, vitally connected to it and bringing our life to the celebrations of the Eucharist, is what it means to live eucharistically.

The Joy of . . . Ministry Series™

THE JOY OF BEING
A EUCHARISTIC MINISTER
Mitch Finley

"... provides insights meant to deepen one's relationship to the risen Christ." —*St. Anthony Messenger*

No. RP 010/04—ISBN 978-1-878718-45-7　　**$5.95**

THE JOY OF PREACHING
Father Rod Damico

"This small book is a gem and should be read by every deacon and candidate." —*Deacon Jerry Wilson*

No. RP 142/04—ISBN 978-1-878718-61-7　　**$6.95**

THE JOY OF BEING A LECTOR
Mitch Finley

"... practical, full of useful suggestions on how to be a better lector." —*Fr. Joseph Champlin*

No. RP 123/04—ISBN 978-1-878718-57-0　　**$5.95**

THE JOY OF BEING AN ALTAR SERVER
Joseph M. Champlin

"Bar none, it's the best little book around for today's altar servers" —*Mitch Finley*

No. RP 162/04—ISBN 978-1-878718-66-2　　**$5.95**

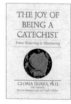

THE JOY OF BEING A CATECHIST
Gloria Durka, Ph.D.

"Chock full of suggestions both practical and spiritual for gaining or maintaining our visions." —*Religion Teachers Journal*

No. RP 520/04—ISBN 978-1-878718-27-3　　**$4.95**

THE JOY OF USHERS AND
HOSPITALITY MINISTERS
Sr. Gretchen Hailer, RSHM

In eight short chapters, parish hospitality ministers share ways to make your parish a place of Welcome.

No. RP 328/04—ISBN 978-1-878718-60-0　　**$5.95**

www.catholicbookpublishing.com

HEALING THROUGH THE MASS
Robert DeGrandis

"... this fine book will be of great help to you and your loved ones." —*Bishop Paul V. Dudley*

No. RP 090/04—ISBN 978-1-878718-10-5   **$8.95**

CATHOLIC IS WONDERFUL!
How to Make the Most of It
Mitch Finley

"Finley's enthusiasm and appreciation for the Catholic faith makes this a book every teacher will treasure."
—*Bill Griffin*

No. RP 440/04—ISBN 978-1-878718-24-2   **$4.95**

NINE HABITS OF
HIGHLY EFFECTIVE CHRISTIANS
Victor M. Parachin

"Parachin's easy-to-read primer on how to be a better Christian is filled with anecdotes, examples, and tips for Christian action and has something for everyone." —*Marci Alborghetti*

No. RP 757/04—ISBN 978-1-933066-11-0   **$6.95**

LIFE, LOVE AND LAUGHTER
The Spirituality of the Consciousness Examen
Father Jim Vlaun

"... There is so much simple, shining wisdom in this book."
—*William J. O'Malley, S.J.*

No. RP 113/04—ISBN 978-1-878718-43-3   **$7.95**

FEASTS OF LIFE
Recipes from Nana's Wooden Spoon
Father Jim Vlaun

"Filled with wonderful stories and even better-sounding recipes ... easy to make and don't require fancy ingredients. Includes a prayer for grace, a cooking equivalents table and a cross-referenced index." —*Crux of the News*

No. RP 168/04—ISBN 978-1-878718-76-1   **$12.95**

www.catholicbookpublishing.com

Additional Titles Published by Resurrection Press, a Catholic Book Publishing Imprint

For a free catalog call 1-800-892-6657
www.catholicbookpublishing.com